285 Ultimate Baked Potato Recipes

(285 Ultimate Baked Potato Recipes - Volume 1)

Penny Patton

Copyright: Published in the United States by Penny Patton/ © PENNY PATTON

Published on November, 24 2020

All rights reserved. No part of this publication may be reproduced, stored in retrieval system, copied in any form or by any means, electronic, mechanical, photocopying, recording or otherwise transmitted without written permission from the publisher. Please do not participate in or encourage piracy of this material in any way. You must not circulate this book in any format. PENNY PATTON does not control or direct users' actions and is not responsible for the information or content shared, harm and/or actions of the book readers.

In accordance with the U.S. Copyright Act of 1976, the scanning, uploading and electronic sharing of any part of this book without the permission of the publisher constitute unlawful piracy and theft of the author's intellectual property. If you would like to use material from the book (other than just simply for reviewing the book), prior permission must be obtained by contacting the author at author@fetarecipes.com

Thank you for your support of the author's rights.

195. Leahs Baked Scalloped Potatoes Au Gratin Recipe 89
196. Lemon Baked Potatoes Recipe 90
197. Lemon Lime Baked Sweet Potatoes Recipe 90
198. Loaded Baked Potato Pizza Recipe 91
199. Loaded Baked Potato Recipe 91
200. Loaded Baked Potato Salad Recipe............ 91
201. Loaded Baked Potatoes Recipe 92
202. Loaded Mashed Potato Bake Recipe 92
203. Low Carb Baked Potatoes Recipe 92
204. MASHED NEW POTATO CHEESE BAKE WITH GARLIC Recipe 93
205. Marinated Potatoes Recipe 93
206. Mashed Potato And Gravy Bake Recipe ... 94
207. Mashed Potato Bake Recipe 94
208. Mashed Potato Layer Bake Recipe 94
209. Mashed Potatoes Baked With Cream Recipe 95
210. Mexican Baked Potatoes Recipe 95
211. Microwave Dill Baked Potatoe Salad Recipe 95
212. Mini Baked Potatoes With Blue Cheese Recipe 96
213. Mint & Sumac Rustic Potatoes Recipe....... 96
214. Moose And Potato Bake Recipe 97
215. Mushroom Filler For Baked Potato Recipe 97
216. Mustard Aioli Baked Potatoes With Herbs Recipe 97
217. Never Eat Another Potato But This One! Recipe 98
218. New Baked Potatoes Recipe 98
219. Nothing To It Baked Potato Restaurant Style Recipe.. 98
220. One Pan Chicken And Potato Bake Recipe 99
221. Oven Baked Potato Wedges Recipe 99
222. Oven Baked Potatoes Recipe 99
223. Over Stuffed Chili Baked Potatoes Recipe 100
224. POTATO BAKE Recipe........................... 100
225. Potato Bake Recipe 101
226. Potato Wedges Recipe................................ 101
227. Potato And Ham Bake Recipe................... 101
228. Potatoes Baked With Creamy Eggs Recipe 102
229. Potatoes Ham Bake Recipe....................... 102
230. Quick Fake Baked Potatos With Crispy Skin Recipe.. 103
231. Re Baked Potatoes Recipe 103
232. Reuben Baked Potatoes Recipe 104
233. Roasted Cajun Potatoes Recipe 104
234. Rosemary Garlic Garnished Baked Potatoes Recipe 105
235. Ruben Stuffed Baked Potatoes Recipe ... 105
236. Salmon Stuffed Baked Potatoes Recipe.. 105
237. Salt Baked Potatoes With Roasted Garlic Butter Recipe 106
238. Sausage Stuffed Baked Potatoes Recipe . 106
239. Savory Potato Bake Dated 1962 Recipe . 107
240. Scampi Baked Potato Recipe 107
241. Shake N Bake Potatos Recipe 108
242. Sliced Baked Potatoes Microwaved Recipe 108
243. Sliced Baked Potatoes Recipe................... 108
244. Slow Cooker Cheesy Tuna Baked Potatoes Recipe 109
245. Smashed Potatoes A Flip On Baked Potatoes Recipe 109
246. Smoked 'taters Recipe 110
247. Smoked Cheese Filler For Baked Potato Recipe 110
248. Smoked Fish Filler For Baked Potato Recipe.. 110
249. Special Baked Potatoes Recipe 110
250. Spiced Baked Potatoes Recipe 111
251. Spinach Mashed Potatoes Recipe 111
252. Spinach Potato Cakes Recipe 111
253. Spinach And Cheese Baked Potatoes Recipe 112
254. Stuffed Baked Sweet Potatoes Recipe 112
255. Stuffed Potato Skins Recipe 113
256. Sweet Potato Apple Bake Recipe............. 113
257. Sweet Potato Bake Recipe........................ 114
258. Sweet Potato Berry Bake Recipe............. 114
259. Sweet Potato Pineapple Bake Recipe...... 114
260. Sweet Potatoes In Crockpot Recipe........ 115
261. Taco Tater Skins Recipe 115
262. The Best Sour Cream Your Baked Potato Will Ever Meet Recipe 115
263. Tiny Baked New Potatoes Recipe 116
264. Tuna Baked Potatoes Recipe 116
265. Turkey Potato Bake Recipe 116

127. Better Than Fries! Baked Potatoes Recipe 61
128. Boston Baked Potatoes Recipe 62
129. Broccoli Cheese Potato Bake Recipe 62
130. Brocoli And Bacon Baked Potato Recipe . 62
131. Buffalo Potatoes Recipe 63
132. CARIBBEAN STYLE SPICY BAKED POTATOES Recipe 63
133. Candied Baked Sweet Potato And Apples Recipe 63
134. Caramelized Onion Stuffed Baked Potatoes Recipe 64
135. Cheddar Baked Potato Slices Recipe 65
136. Cheddar Potato Bake Recipe 65
137. Cheese Potato And Onion Bake Recipe ... 65
138. Cheese Sauced Baked Potatoes Recipe 66
139. Cheesy Baked Potato Surprise Recipe 66
140. Chicken & Potato Bake Recipe 66
141. Chicken Potato Enchilada Bake Recipe 67
142. Chicken Sausage And Potato Bake Recipe 67
143. Chili Baked Potato Recipe 68
144. Chilli Seasoned Potato Wedges Recipe 68
145. Chive And Garlic Potato Bake Recipe 68
146. Chorizo And Cheese Baked Potatoes Recipe 69
147. Clam And Potato Bake Recipe 69
148. Colcannon Stuffed Baked Potatoes Recipe 69
149. Country Potato Pancakes 70
150. Country Style Potato Bake Recipe 70
151. Creamy Baked Potatoes Recipe 71
152. Creamy Mashed Potato Bake Recipe 71
153. Creamy Potato Bake Recipe 71
154. Creamy Potato Gratin With Attitude Recipe 71
155. Creamy Red Potatoes Recipe 72
156. Crispy Baked Potato Wedges With Cajun Aioli Recipe 72
157. Crispy Crust Baked Potatoes Recipe 73
158. Crockpot Baked Potato Recipe 73
159. Crump Topped Sour Cream Cheesy Potato Bake Recipe 74
160. Crunchy Blue Cheese And Walnut Filled Baked Potatoes Recipe 74
161. DOUBLE BAKED STUFFED POTATOES Recipe 74
162. Damn Hot Peppers With Potato Hash With Baked Eggs Recipe 75

163. Delicious Chicken Bake With Potato Crust Recipe 75
164. Dijon Baked Potatoes With Cheese And Bacon Aka Twice Baked Recipe 76
165. Double Baked Mashed Potatoes With Fontina And Italian Parsley Recipe 76
166. Double Baked Potato With Low Fat Yogurt And Crispy Onions Recipe 77
167. Double Baked Sardine Potatoes Recipe 77
168. Easter Mashed Baked Potatos Recipe 78
169. Easy Baked Chicken Potatoes And Carrots Recipe 78
170. Easy Cheesy Potatoes Recipe 78
171. Ever So Slightly Sweet Potato Cashew Bake Recipe 79
172. Favorite Macaroni And Cheese Recipe 79
173. Feta Cheese Filler For Baked Potato Recipe 80
174. Fish Fillets Baked With Potatoes Recipe ... 80
175. Fondant Potatoes Recipe 80
176. Fragrant Chicken And Potato Bake Recipe 81
177. French Onion Potato Bake Recipe 81
178. Fresh Filler For Baked Potato Recipe 82
179. Fried Japaleno Sliced Peppers Recipe 82
180. GUADALAJARA BAKED POTATOES Recipe 82
181. Garden Stuffed Baked Potatoes Recipe 83
182. Garlic Baked Potatoes Recipe 83
183. Gotta Be Ultimate Double Baked Potato Boats Recipe 83
184. Greek Potato Bake Recipe 84
185. Grilled Baked Potatoes Recipe 84
186. Ham And Cheese Potato Bake Recipe 85
187. Hasselback Potatoes With Seasoned Breadcrumbs Recipe..................................... 85
188. Herb And Onion Baked Potatoes Recipe . 86
189. Home Style Turkey And Potato Bake Recipe 86
190. Honey Butter Baked Chicken With Mashed Sweet Potatoes Recipe 87
191. In A Hurry But Yummy Potato Bake Recipe 87
192. Italian Potato Topped Chicken Bake Recipe 88
193. Killer Baked Sweet Potatoes Recipe 88
194. Killer Italian Baked Potatoes Recipe 89

61. BAKED NEW POTATO SALAD WITH PEANUTS AND MUSTARD Recipe 35
62. BEER BATTER BAKED POTATOES Recipe 36
63. BEER BAKED SCALLOPED POTATOES Recipe 36
64. Baby Bake Potatoes W Bleu Cheese Topping Recipe 37
65. Bacon Wrapped Potatoes Recipe 37
66. Bake Sweet Potatoes W African Style Peanut Sauce Recipe 37
67. Baked Apples With Sweet Potato Stuffing Recipe 38
68. Baked Bacon Wrapped New Potatoes Recipe 38
69. Baked Carrots And Potatoes Recipe 38
70. Baked Carrots And Potatoes With Nutmeg Recipe 39
71. Baked Chicken Breasts And Potatoes Recipe 39
72. Baked Dill Potatoes Recipe 40
73. Baked Eggs In Potato Recipe 40
74. Baked Eggs In Potatoes Recipe 41
75. Baked German Potato Salad Recipe 41
76. Baked New Potato Salad With Peanuts And Mustard Dressing Recipe 42
77. Baked New Red Potatoes Recipe 42
78. Baked Old Bay Potato Sticks Recipe 42
79. Baked Potato Bar Recipe 43
80. Baked Potato Discs Recipe 43
81. Baked Potato Eggs Recipe 44
82. Baked Potato Hint Recipe 44
83. Baked Potato Pizza Recipe 44
84. Baked Potato Recipe 45
85. Baked Potato Salad Recipe 45
86. Baked Potato Skins Like TGIFridays And Ruby Tuesdays Recipe 45
87. Baked Potato Skins Recipe 46
88. Baked Potato Slims Recipe 46
89. Baked Potato Taco Recipe 47
90. Baked Potato Wedges Recipe 47
91. Baked Potato With Vegetable Soup Recipe 47
92. Baked Potato And Cheese Balls Recipe 48
93. Baked Potato Bacon And Chives Bread Recipe 48
94. Baked Potatoe Strips Recipe 49

95. Baked Potatoes Simply Become Salad Recipe 49
96. Baked Potatoes Stuffed With Spinach Parmesan And Mushrooms Recipe 50
97. Baked Potatoes Stuffed With Bacon Anchovies And Sage Recipe 50
98. Baked Potatoes Stuffed With Crabmeat Recipe 51
99. Baked Potatoes With Olives And Feta Recipe 51
100. Baked Potatoes On The Grill Recipe 51
101. Baked Potatoes With Cornmeal Recipe 52
102. Baked Potatoes With Dreams Of Glory Recipe 52
103. Baked Rosti Potatoes Recipe 52
104. Baked Spanish Potato Omelet Recipe 53
105. Baked Spicy Ham And Cheese Mashed Potatoes Recipe 53
106. Baked Stuffed New Potatoes Recipe 53
107. Baked Sweet Potato Chips Recipe 54
108. Baked Sweet Potato Felafel Recipe 54
109. Baked Sweet Potato Latkes Recipe 55
110. Baked Sweet Potato Recipe 55
111. Baked Sweet Potato With Cinnamon Chile Butter Recipe 55
112. Baked Sweet Potato And Chile Wedges Recipe 56
113. Baked Sweet Potatoes Recipe 56
114. Baked Sweet Potatoes With Bacon And Blue Cheese Recipe 57
115. Baked Sweet Potatoes With Ginger And Honey Recipe 57
116. Baked Tex Mex Potato With Pico Degallo Recipe 57
117. Baked Tomatoes Stuffed With Cheesy Potatoes Recipe 58
118. Baked White Fish And Fingerling Potatoes Recipe 58
119. Baked Potato Salad Recipe 59
120. Baked Potatoes In The Crockpot Recipe .. 59
121. Baked Potatoes With Apple Recipe 59
122. Baked Potatoes With Cheese Cream Recipe 60
123. Baked Spiraled Garlic Potatoes Recipe 60
124. Balsamic Baked Potatoes Recipe 60
125. Beefy Spicy Baked Potatoes Recipe 61
126. Best Simplest Baked Potato Recipe 61

Content

CHAPTER 1: TWICE BAKED POTATO RECIPES 8

1. Awesome Twice Baked Potatoes Recipe 8
2. Baked Or Twice Baked Potato Recipe 8
3. Cheesy Twice Baked Potatoes Recipe 8
4. Cheesy Twice Baked Potatoes With Onion Sauce Recipe 9
5. Cheesy Twice Baked Potatoes With Mushrooms Recipe 10
6. Crab Stuffed Twice Baked Potatoes Recipe 10
7. Crock Pot Stuffed Potatoes Recipe............. 11
8. Easy Egg Twice Baked Potatoe Recipe...... 11
9. Easy Twice Baked Potato Bits Recipe 12
10. Garden Stuffed Potatoes Recipe 12
11. Ground Beef And Twice Baked Potato Pie Recipe 13
12. Healthy Twice Baked Potato Skins Recipe 13
13. Herbed Twice Baked Potatoes Recipe 13
14. Loaded Stuffed Baked Potatoes Recipe 14
15. Loaded Twice Baked Potatoes Recipe 14
16. Loaded Twice Baked Potatoes Recipe 15
17. Lobster Stuffed Baked Potato With Spinach Recipe 15
18. Pink Stuffed Potatoes Recipe 16
19. Reuben Twice Baked Potatoes Recipe 17
20. Roasted Jalapeno Twice Baked Potatoes Recipe 17
21. Smoked Bacon Cheddar Twice Baked Potatoes Recipe 18
22. Southern Twice Baked Potatoes Recipe ... 18
23. Southwest Stuffed Twice Baked Spuds Recipe 18
24. Spicy Chili Stuffed Twice Baked Potatoes Recipe 19
25. Stuffed Baked Potatoes Recipe 20
26. TWICE BAKED POTATOES Recipe 20
27. TWICE BAKED YUKON GOLD POTATO WITH GOAT CHEESE And Rosemary Recipe 20
28. Tuna Stuffed Twice Baked Potato Recipe 21
29. Twice Baked Potato Recipe 21
30. Twice Baked Potatoes Recipe 22
31. Twice Baked Potatoes In A Slow Cooker Recipe 22
32. Twice Baked Potatoes With Alouette Cheese Recipe 23
33. Twice Baked Potatoes With Broccoli Recipe 23
34. Twice Baked Potatoes With Chili And Cheese Recipe 23
35. Twice Baked Ranch Potatoes Recipe 24
36. Twice Baked Red Potatoes With Roasted Jalapeno Recipe 24
37. Twice Baked Sweet Potatoes Recipe 25
38. Twice Baked Sweet Potatoes With A Flare" Recipe 25
39. Twice Baked White Cheddar Sage Potatoes Recipe 25
40. Twice Baked Yams Recipe 26
41. Twice Smashed Baked Potatoes Recipe 26
42. Twice Baked Potato Chicken Pot Pie Recipe 27
43. Twice Baked Potatoes Recipe 27
44. Twice Baked Mashed Potatoes Recipe 28
45. Twice Baked Potato Skins W Pepperoni Recipe 28
46. Twice Baked Stuffed Potatoes Recipe 28
47. Twice Baked Buttermilk Potatoes Recipe . 29
48. Twice Baked Spinach Potatoes Recipe 29
49. Twiced Baked New Potatoes Recipe 30
50. Ultimate Twice Baked Potatoes Recipe..... 30
51. Veggie Marscapone Twice Baked Potatoes Recipe 31
52. Veggie Twice Baked Potatoes Recipe 31
53. Yams Twice Baked Recipe 31
54. Twice Baked Onion Potatoes Recipe 32
55. Twice Baked Potato Sheet Cake Recipe 32
56. Twice Baked Potatoes Recipe 33
57. Twice Baked Potatoes Master Recipe Recipe 33

CHAPTER 2: AWESOME BAKED POTATO RECIPES 34

58. Alpine Potato Bake Recipe 34
59. Apple Sweet Potato Bake Recipe 34
60. B Grill Chili Cheese Stuffed Baked Potato Recipe 35

266. Tuscan Cheese Potato Bake Recipe 117
267. Two Potatoe Baked Cassarole Recipe 117
268. Ukranaian Potato Bake Dated 1967 Recipe 117
269. Ultimate Baked Potato Recipe 118
270. VeggieStuffed Baked Potato Recipe 118
271. Volcano Potatoe Bake Recipe 119
272. Whipped Sweet Potato Bake Recipe........119
273. Yummy Asparagus Potato Ham Bake Recipe 119
274. Zooming In Potato Bake Recipe 120
275. Zucchini Potato Bake Recipe 120
276. Baked Mashed Potatoes Extreme Recipe 121
277. Baked Potato Recipe..................................121
278. Baked Potato Topping Recipe 121
279. Baked Potatoe Collins Style Recipe 121
280. Baked Whipped Cheezy Potatoes Recipe 122
281. Caramalised Onion And Cheese Potato Bake Recipe 122
282. Cheesy Potato And Ham Bake Recipe 123
283. Cheesy Potato Bake Recipe 123
284. Garlic Lovers Baked Potato Recipe 123
285. Ham And Cheese Potato Bake Recipe 124

INDEX **125**
CONCLUSION **128**

Chapter 1: Twice Baked Potato Recipes

***

1. Awesome Twice Baked Potatoes Recipe

Serving: 1 | Prep: | Cook: 15mins | Ready in:

Ingredients

- One Large Baking potato
- 1/4 C Shredded cheese, your preference
- 1 tsp. Ranch seasoning Mix
- 2 Tbsp. sour cream
- Optional: green onion

Direction

- Wash potato thoroughly.
- Bake in microwave or in oven (microwave is usually 5-8 min. depending on wattage. Be sure to poke holes in the potato before you cook!)
- Allow potato to cool slightly.
- Cut in half and scoop out insides, not going completely to the skin.
- Mash inside of potato with sour cream and ranch seasoning until smooth (if you need more seasoning or sour cream add it!).
- Spoon potato mixture back into potato skins.
- Top with cheese and broil for 10 minutes or until cheese is bubbly.
- Serve with sour cream and green onion.

2. Baked Or Twice Baked Potato Recipe

Serving: 4 | Prep: | Cook: 45mins | Ready in:

Ingredients

- For a baked potato, I wash & poke holes in it with a fork, coat the outside with bacon grease or olive oil and S&P to taste (this makes the tater skins delicious). Grill indirect or smoke until tender.

Direction

- For twice baked potatoes, follow directions above and when the potatoes are tender, remove and cut in half lengthwise. Carefully scoop out the potato from its skin leaving a little potato attached to the skin to help it hold its shape. Mash the potatoes and mix in some or all:
- Shredded cheese
- Sour cream
- Crispy bacon bits or ham chunks
- Butter
- Finely chopped jalapenos
- Horseradish
- Chopped onion
- Chives
- Salt and pepper
- (Basically anything you'd see on a potato bar)
- Mix the ingredients and spoon back into the potato skin shells (heaping over a bit) then return to cooker until filling is hot, cheese melts and potato begins to brown.

3. Cheesy Twice Baked Potatoes Recipe

Serving: 4 | Prep: | Cook: 60mins | Ready in:

Ingredients

- 2 large baking potaotes, scrubbed and rinsed
- 4 slices thick cut bacon, diced into 1 inch pieces
- 1 tablespoon butter
- 1/4 cup milk
- 1/4 cup sour cream
- 1/2 cup grated cheddar cheese, plus about 1/4 cup more for topping
- 1/2 cup grated pepper jack cheese
- 2 green onions, diced about 2 tablespoons

Direction

- Preheat oven to 400 degrees. Puncture potatoes with a fork about 6 times around the potato, this will allow steam to escape while they are cooking. Bake for 50-60 minutes or until the skins are crispy but the potato is soft. You should be able to insert a fork and remove it easily.
- While your potato is cooking cook your bacon until brown. Remove to paper towel lined plate. Set aside.
- Once your potatoes are baked, turn your oven down to 350 degrees.
- Slice the potatoes in half lengthwise (Note: be careful they will retain a lot of the heat for a while). Being careful not to puncture the skin, spoon out the insides, place them in a mixing bowl and set the skins aside.
- To the potatoes add butter, milk and sour cream. Use an electric mixer and mix until smooth. Stir in 1/2 cup cheddar cheese, pepper jack cheese and green onions. Mix well.
- Fill the potato skins with the mixture. Top with remaining cheddar cheese.
- Bake at 350 degrees in a baking dish until the cheese melts.

4. Cheesy Twice Baked Potatoes With Onion Sauce Recipe

Serving: 4 | Prep: | Cook: 60mins | Ready in:

Ingredients

- POTATOES:
- 8 pieces bacon, cooked and crumbled
- 4 lg. baking potatoes
- 1 tbsp. butter
- 4 tbsp. half & half
- 1 egg yolk, beaten
- 1/4 tsp. black pepper
- 1/2 c. grated Swiss or brick cheese
- 1/4 c. parmesan cheese
- onion SAUCE:
- 2 T green onion, minced
- 2 T butter
- 2 T All-purpose flour
- 1/2 c milk
- 1/2 c half and half

Direction

- POTATOES:
- Preheat oven to 450
- Scrub and dry potatoes.
- Prick with a fork and rub with butter.
- Bake about 1 hour or until tender.
- Cook bacon, drain and crumble
- Cut a slice from the top of each potato.
- Scoop out pulp into a bowl.
- Mash the potatoes until free from lumps.
- Beat in the butter, half and half and egg yolk.
- Stir in black pepper and cheese.
- Refill potato shells.
- Make a well in the potatoes.
- Sprinkle with crumbled bacon
- Fill with the sauce.
- Sprinkle with Parmesan cheese.
- Broil until browned.
- ONION SAUCE:
- Sauté 2 tablespoons minced green onions in 2 tablespoons butter. Add 2 tablespoons all-purpose flour. Cook 1 minute.
- Slowly pour in 1/2 cup each milk and half and half, stirring constantly. Salt to taste.
- Cook until thickened.

5. Cheesy Twice Baked Potatoes With Mushrooms Recipe

Serving: 4 | Prep: | Cook: 90mins | Ready in:

Ingredients

- 4 medium-sized baking potatoes
- 2 Tbsp butter
- milk
- salt and pepper
- 2 ounce can chopped mushrooms
- 2 slices American cheese
- paprika

Direction

- Bake potatoes by your preferred method of baking potatoes then let them cool until you can handle them.
- Cut a slice from the top of each potato.
- On your slices, carefully peel off the skin and discard. Place the potato slices in a bowl.
- Use a spoon to carefully scoop the potato out of the inside of your baked potatoes, just leaving a thin shell of potato and peel.
- Add the potato you scoop out to the potato slices in the bowl and set aside your potato shells.
- Using a potato masher, mash the potatoes in the bowl with the butter and just enough milk to make a stiff consistency.
- Add salt and pepper to taste.
- Drain the mushrooms and carefully stir them into the mashed potato mixture, without breaking up the mushrooms.
- Divide the mashed potato mixture into four portions and fill the potato shells with it.
- Place your filled potatoes in an 11x7 baking dish.
- Bake at 425 for 20 minutes or so, until potato filling is lightly browned.
- Slice each cheese slice in half diagonally. Place one cheese triangle on top of each filled potato.
- Sprinkle with paprika and return to oven for 2 or 3 minutes, just long enough to melt the cheese.
- Serve immediately.

6. Crab Stuffed Twice Baked Potatoes Recipe

Serving: 6 | Prep: | Cook: 15mins | Ready in:

Ingredients

- 3 large baking potatoes
- 1/2 cup more or less sour cream
- 1/4 stick butter
- 1 jalapeno pepper minced
- 1 clove garlic minced
- 2 green onions sliced thin
- 1 tsp kosher salt
- 3 turns of black pepper mill
- 1/2 cup mozzarella cheese cut VERY small pieces
- 1/2 to 1 cup minced lump meat crab

Direction

- You can micro potatoes however I find oven baking gives a firmer skin
- Bake remove from oven and cool slightly
- Remove potato from skins and place in bowl
- Mash roughly and add crab and cheese and fluff with fork
- In heated pan melt butter and add pepper onion and garlic; salt and pepper
- Cook just until softened
- Add to potato/crab mixture
- Mix gently
- Place mixture in the six potato skins
- Heat oven to 325
- Place potatoes on cookie sheet and heat in oven
- Serve with dollop of sour cream on top with fresh chopped parsley (optional)

7. Crock Pot Stuffed Potatoes Recipe

Serving: 0 | Prep: | Cook: 8hours7mins | Ready in:

Ingredients

- 5-6 lg baking potatoes
- 3 TBS butter
- 1/2 cup milk
- 1/2 cup sour cream
- 1 tsp salt
- 1/8 tsp pepper
- 2 TBS grated parmesan cheese
- chopped chives

Direction

- Wash potatoes; do not dry. Place into slow cooker; cover and cook on low 6-8 hrs. or until tender. Remove from pot. Cut a thick slice lengthwise from the top of each potato. Scoop hot pulp into mixing bowl, saving the potato shell to fill later.
- To the potato pulp add butter, milk, sour cream, salt and pepper. Beat until fluffy, adding more milk if necessary. Spoon mixture into shells, mounding tops. Sprinkle with cheese. Place in shallow baking pan. Bake at 425 for 15 minutes, or until hot and lightly browned. Top with chopped chives.

8. Easy Egg Twice Baked Potatoe Recipe

Serving: 2 | Prep: | Cook: 90mins | Ready in:

Ingredients

- The spuds:
- 2 large potatoes (around 250g each), preferably a floury variety
- olive oil
- coarse salt
- The rest:
- olive oil for frying
- 1 small onion (around 75g), finely chopped
- 1 clove garlic, finely chopped
- 1 tsp chopped fresh tarragon
- coarse salt to taste
- freshly ground black pepper to taste
- 1-2 tsp extra virgin olive oil
- 2 eggs
- 1 tblsp grated parmesan

Direction

- The Steps:
- Preheat your oven to 200C
- Scrub the potatoes and dry them. Prick the skin all over using a fork or small knife and brush with olive oil.
- Sprinkle a baking tray with some coarse salt, place the potatoes on the tray and bake until tender, which should take somewhere between an hour and an hour and a quarter, depending on size.
- While the potatoes are baking, place a small frying pan over a medium heat. When hot, add some olive oil, enough to coat the pan.
- Add the onions to the pan. Stir and fry for around 10 minutes or until they are starting to brown around the edges.
- Add the garlic and chopped tarragon to the pan, along with a couple of twists of black pepper and a pinch of salt. Stir and fry for another 2 minutes or so and remove from the heat.
- When the potatoes are done, remove from the oven (but leave the oven turned on). Allow the potatoes to cool for a few minutes, then cut each one in half and scoop out the cooked flesh, being careful not to pierce the skins.
- Mash the cooked potato lightly with a fork and mix in the fried onion. Add coarse salt and freshly ground black pepper to taste, along with a tsp. or two of some extra virgin olive oil, again to taste.
- Use a few tbsp. of the potato mixture to line two of the potato halves with a mashed potato layer.

- Now, take one of the eggs and crack it into a small bowl or jug. Then pour the egg into one of the lined potato shells. If your potato is not big enough for the entire egg, you may need to keep back some of the egg white. Repeat with the second egg.
- Divide the remaining potato mixture between the two other potato halves, piling them high.
- Sprinkle the lot with the parmesan and return to the oven for 10-15 minutes, or until the whites of the eggs are set. Then eat.
- Variations
- You could use parsley, chives or thyme instead of tarragon when frying the onions and you could add bits of bacon, ham or sausage If you like and/or mix some sour cream or butter into the potato instead of the olive oil.

9. Easy Twice Baked Potato Bits Recipe

Serving: 2 | Prep: | Cook: 15mins | Ready in:

Ingredients

- As many potatoes as you need
- diced onions to taste
- ranch dressing
- sea salt and fresh cracked pepper to taste
- Shredded sharp cheddar cheese or whatever kind of cheese you prefer

Direction

- How many small potatoes that you need.
- Wash potatoes, with skins on, and wrap in paper towels.
- Cook in microwave until soft.
- Preheat oven to 325 degrees and loosely wrap potatoes in foil and put in oven until skins crisp up.
- Let cool then scoop out making sure not to break skins.
- With a potatoes masher, mix scooped out potatoes, onion and Ranch Dressing until it is the consistency you like.
- Stuff skins with mixture and sprinkle liberally with cheese.
- Wrap in foil and place back in oven until cheese melts.
- Enjoy!!!!!!!!!!
- We also use this same recipe for large potatoes.

10. Garden Stuffed Potatoes Recipe

Serving: 4 | Prep: | Cook: 30mins | Ready in:

Ingredients

- 4 large russet potatoes, scrubbed
- 2 tbsp butter
- 1 small onion, chopped
- 2 cups of broccoli, chopped
- 1/2 c ranch dressing
- 1 tbsp vegetable oil
- 2 tsp parsley, chopped
- 2/3 c sharp cheddar, shredded

Direction

- Preheat oven to 425F. Pierce potatoes and microwave on high for 10-12 minutes. Wrap in foil and bake for 10 minutes. Unwrap and slice potatoes in half. Scoop out potatoes, leaving jacket. Mash pulp. Sauté onion in butter for a few minutes. Add broccoli and sauté for a few minutes. Remove from heat and add salad dressing. Next add potatoes pulp. Brush potato jackets with oil. Spoon potato mixture into jacket, top with cheese and baked for 10 minutes until cheese melts. Sprinkle with salt, pepper and parsley.

11. Ground Beef And Twice Baked Potato Pie Recipe

Serving: 4 | Prep: | Cook: 50mins | Ready in:

Ingredients

- 1.5 lb lean ground beef (I use 93%)
- 1/4 c chopped onion
- 1/4 c Progresso plain bread crumbs
- 1/2 t dried sage
- 1/2 t seasoned alt
- 1/2 t garlic pepper
- 2 T worcestershire sauce
- 2 t chopped garlic
- 1 egg
- 1 package (1lb 8 oz) refrigerated garlic mashed potatoes (I used leftover mashed)
- 1 c shredded cheese (I use the 4 flavor casserole melt)
- 1 c chopped fresh tomato
- 1 slices bacon, cooked and chopped
- 2 T chopped green onion
- 4 T sour cream

Direction

- Heat oven to 350
- In a large bowl, mix beef, onion, bread crumbs, sage, seasoned salt, garlic pepper, Worcestershire, garlic and egg until well blended
- Press in bottom of ungreased 8-inch square (2 qt.) glass baking dish
- Spread mashed potatoes over top
- Cover with cheese
- Bake uncovered about 50 minutes, or until meat thermometer inserted in centre reads 160
- Sprinkle with tomato, bacon and green onions
- Top servings with 1 T sour cream

12. Healthy Twice Baked Potato Skins Recipe

Serving: 1 | Prep: | Cook: 120mins | Ready in:

Ingredients

- Baking size potatoes, washed, skin on.
- 1 cooked, diced chicken breast (seasoned as you prefer)
- turkey bacon (4 slices per spud, 2 slices on each half)
- Finely shredded cheese, your favorite (I use cheddar)
- Your favorite condiments, i.e veggies, salsa, sour cream, herbs, spices, etc.

Direction

- Bake the spuds until they are done.
- Allow to cool enough to handle, so you can cut the spuds in half and scoop out the potato flesh. Meanwhile, put the turkey bacon in the over to cook (suggested temp of 350, monitored).
- Once hollowed, line the skins with 2 slices of the cooked turkey bacon.
- Fill with some of the chicken.
- Sprinkle with the shredded cheese (add any spices, herbs, or veggies you want cooked).
- Bake at 350 for about 20 - 30 minutes.
- Serve as is or topped with your favourite condiments.

13. Herbed Twice Baked Potatoes Recipe

Serving: 4 | Prep: | Cook: 1hours30mins | Ready in:

Ingredients

- 2 medium baking potatoes
- 1 1/2 ounces reduced-fat cream cheese, cubed
- 1 tablespoon snipped chives
- 1/4 teaspoon salt

- 1/4 teaspoon dried basil
- dash cayenne pepper
- 3 tablespoons fat-free milk
- 3 teaspoons butter, melted and divided
- 1 dash garlic powder
- 1 dash paprika

Direction

- Scrub and pierce potatoes. Bake at 375 degrees F for 1 hour or until tender. Cool for 10 minutes. Cut potatoes in half. Scoop out pulp, leaving a thin shell.
- In a bowl, mash the pulp with cream cheese, chives, salt, basil and cayenne. Add milk and 1-1/2 teaspoons butter; mash. Spoon into potato shells. Drizzle with remaining butter; sprinkle with garlic powder and paprika. Place on an ungreased baking sheet. Bake for 15-20 minutes or until heated through.

14. Loaded Stuffed Baked Potatoes Recipe

Serving: 4 | Prep: | Cook: 85mins | Ready in:

Ingredients

- 4 large baking potatoes (ex idaho Russets, or thick skinned variety)
- olive oil to the skins
- sour cream, start with 1/2 cup
- cream cheese, start with 4 oz
- butter, start with 1/4 cup
- milk or half and half, start with 1/4 cup
- sharp cheddar cheese, start with 1 Pkg.
- green onions or chives , start with 1 bunch chopped (green parts)
- chopped cooked bacon, start with 6 strips
- salt, pepper or BBQ seasoning,cajun spice etc

Direction

- Wash potatoes
- Pat completely dry
- Rub skin with olive oil
- Bake uncovered (no foil) from 350-400F about 1 hour or tested done when top pricked with a fork
- When warm enough to handle hollow out:
- Scoop out potato, leaving at least 1/4 inch or some potato left on the sides and bottom so skin remains intact
- Now to the scooped out potato:
- Mash and add in the cream cheese, sour cream and butter to taste.
- Add enough milk to loosen mixture if needed to desired texture
- Season liberally to taste.
- Stuff mixture into potato shells
- Now here are variations of preparation:
- Either top with the green onions, cooked chopped bacon or cover with cheese
- Bake additional 15 minutes at 350F
- OR simply mix in "some "of the green onion, bacon and shredded cheese and top with remainder of bacon, onion and cheese and bake the additional 15 minutes.
- Note: other variations: other cheeses, crumbled cooked sausage, sautéed mushrooms, chopped cooked broccoli, caramelized onions,

15. Loaded Twice Baked Potatoes Recipe

Serving: 4 | Prep: | Cook: 10mins | Ready in:

Ingredients

- 4 medium russet potatoes
- 8 ounces ground beef
- 1 cup broccoli florets, finely chopped
- 1 cup water
- 1 cup cheddar cheese, divided
- 1/2 sour cream
- 1/2 teaspoon salt
- 1/4 teaspoon freshly ground pepper
- 3 scallions, sliced

Direction

- Pierce potatoes all over with a fork.
- Place in the microwave and cook at 50% power, turning once or twice, until the potatoes are soft, about 20 minutes. (Or, use the "potato setting" on your microwave and cook according to the manufacturer's instructions.)
- Meanwhile, brown meat in a large skillet over medium-high heat, stirring often, about 3 minutes.
- Transfer to a large bowl. Increase heat to high, add broccoli and water to the skillet, cover, and cook until tender, 4 to 5 minutes. Drain the broccoli; add to the meat.
- Carefully cut off the top third of the cooked potatoes; reserve the tops for another use. Scoop the insides out into a medium bowl. Place the potato shells in a small baking dish.
- Add 1/2 cup Cheddar, sour cream, salt and pepper to the potato insides and mash with a fork or potato masher. Add scallions and the potato mixture to the broccoli and meat; stir to combine.
- Evenly divide the potato mixture among the potato shells and top with the remaining 1/2 cup cheese.
- Microwave on high until the filling is hot and the cheese is melted, 2 to 4 minutes.

16. Loaded Twice Baked Potatoes Recipe

Serving: 3 | Prep: | Cook: 30mins | Ready in:

Ingredients

- 3 lg. baking potatoes
- shortening OR veg. oil
- kosher salt
- 9 slices thick-cut bacon
- 5 oz. sharp cheddar cheese
- 4 T. butter, at room temperature
- 1/2 c. sour cream
- 3/4 tsp. salt
- 1/2 tsp. pepper
- 1/4 tsp. garlic powder

Direction

- Rinse the potatoes and pat dry with paper towels.
- Rub shortening all over potatoes, or roll in vegetable oil; then roll potatoes in kosher salt and place in your baking dish.
- Bake in preheated 400-degree oven until tender, 1 to 1-1/2 hours depending on the size of your spuds. Remove from oven and cool for 20 to 30 minutes.
- While potatoes are baking, cook the bacon until crispy, drain on paper towels, and set aside.
- Slice off the top of each potato and carefully scoop out the centre with a spoon.
- Place scooped-out bits in bowl and mash just to break up. Stir in remaining ingredients, EXCEPT the bacon.
- Spoon the potato mixture back into the potato skins in your baking dish.
- All of the above you can do ahead of time, and at this point you can refrigerate (or wrap and freeze) the stuffed potatoes until ready to use.
- Bake your stuffed potatoes at 350-degrees for 30 minutes. Remove from oven and push broken, crisp bacon into potatoes; place under broiler for a couple of minutes.

17. Lobster Stuffed Baked Potato With Spinach Recipe

Serving: 4 | Prep: | Cook: 1hours30mins | Ready in:

Ingredients

- • 4 large russet baking potatoes, about 3/4 pound each, scrubbed and dried.
- • 1 cup lobster cut into small bite sized bits.
- • 2 strips of smoked bacon, cut into small bits.
- • 3 Tbs. butter.

- • 1 Tbs. olive oil for brushing the spuds.
- • 1/3 cup sour cream.
- • 2 Tbs. parmesan cheese, grated for topping.
- • 1 scallion, finely chopped.
- • ½ tsp. minced garlic. Optional.
- • Spices that please you. For the lobster I used a pinch to a healthy pinch each of oregano, basil, parsley and chopped rosemary. Mix and match to suit yourself.
- • ½ cup thinly sliced fresh mushrooms.
- • 1 cup very thick roux. If you don't know how to make this there are lots of recipes here at GR.
- • 1 small bunch fresh spinach, rinsed and cut crosswise into very fine strips..
- • Salt and FG black pepper.

Direction

- 1. Preheat the oven to 400° F. (200° C).
- 2. Scrub the potatoes well. Dry and brush with olive oil.
- 3. Place the potatoes directly on the rack (rock salt) in the centre of the oven and bake for 30 minutes.
- 4. Pierce each potato in a couple spots with a fork and continue to bake until tender, about 30 more minutes.
- 5. While the potatoes are baking, heat a medium size skillet and began to sauté he bacon. When the bacon has released some oil, add the lobster bits and sauté until the bacon and lobster are just cooked. Set aside. They'll cook a bit more in the potatoes.
- 6. Make the roux, adding spices of choice. When it has thickened, add the thinly sliced mushrooms and spinach and cook another 2-3 minutes. Cover and set aside.
- 7. Remove potatoes from the oven, and turn the heat down to 350° F. (175° C.).
- 8. Hold the potato with an oven-mitt or towel, trim off the top third of the potatoes to make a canoe-like shape. Reserve the tops.
- 9. Carefully scoop out most of the potato into a bowl. Take care to leave enough potato in the skin so the shells stay together.
- 10. Remove about 1-1¼ cup of potato from the bowel and set aside for another use.
- 11. Mash the potato in the bowel lightly with fork along with 2-3 Tbs. of the butter, the spices you've chosen and sour cream. Stir in the scallion, and the lobster mixture and season with salt and pepper, to taste.
- 12. Season the skins with salt and pepper. Refill the shells with the potato/lobster mixture, mounding it slightly. Set the potatoes and lids on a baking sheet (the sauce will drip); spoon the spinach sauce evenly over each potato, sprinkle the cheese on top and bake until heated through, about 20 minutes.
- 13. Serve immediately.
- 14. When you remove the potatoes from baking sheet use a spatula and scoop up any spinach sauce that has run off the potato.
- COOK'S TIP: At step #12 I place the potatoes on medium size, oven proof plates for the final 20 minute bake. All the spinach sauce is there for the taking.

18. Pink Stuffed Potatoes Recipe

Serving: 8 | Prep: | Cook: 1hours45mins | Ready in:

Ingredients

- 4 baking potatoes, pricked with a fork
- 2 medium beets, quartered
- 2 shallots, diced
- 3 cloves garlic, minced
- pinch salt
- black pepper to taste

Direction

- Preheat oven to 375.
- Place potatoes and beets on a cookie sheet and bake for 50-60 minutes, turning over halfway through.
- Remove from the oven and allow to cool slightly, then peel the beets and halve the potatoes, scooping out the insides.

- Place the peeled beets and potato flesh in a bowl (keep the skins) and set aside.
- In a medium non-stick pan, sauté shallot and garlic in a small amount of cooking spray or water until softened, then scrape into the potato mixture.
- Add salt and pepper to taste and mash until smooth.
- Scoop the mashed mixture back into the reserved potato skins.
- Place potatoes back in the oven and bake a further 10 minutes

19. Reuben Twice Baked Potatoes Recipe

Serving: 4 | Prep: | Cook: 15mins | Ready in:

Ingredients

- 4 russet potatoes, pierced, baked and cooled enough to handle
- 2 T. butter
- 1 C. onion, chopped
- 1 1/2 C. sauerkraut, drained
- 1 t. caraway seeds
- 1 C. corned beef, chopped (from the deli)
- 1 C. swiss cheese, shredded (Kraft makes a pre-shredded Swiss)
- 1 T. fresh chives (ehhh, you can leave these off if you don't want the expense - makes them pretty though)
- Russian dressing

Direction

- Lengthwise, cut a 1/2" slice off the potato & set aside. Scoop out potato leaving 1/4" shell & set aside. Place shells on pan. Preheat broiler to high.
- Melt butter in skillet, sauté onions. Add sauerkraut, caraway seeds & reserved scooped potato; mix and heat until mixture begins to brown. Add corned beef. Stir. Add Swiss cheese, stir quickly, and spoon mixture into shells. Top with additional Swiss.
- Broil until cheese is melted and lightly browned. Serve with Russian dressing.
- NOTE: I turn the cut off tops of the potatoes into yummy skins for a snack.

20. Roasted Jalapeno Twice Baked Potatoes Recipe

Serving: 6 | Prep: | Cook: 25mins | Ready in:

Ingredients

- 2 lbs potatoes (small Red or small Yukon Gold)
- 1-2 fresh jalapeno peppers
- 1-1/2 Tb butter
- 1/4 c sour cream
- 2 strips bacon, cooked (or bacon bits)
- 1/3 c grated cheddar cheese
- 1/2 tsp salt
- 1/3 tsp fresh ground pepper
- 2 chopped scallions, green part only

Direction

- Boil potatoes until slightly soft, about 15 mins. Remove potatoes from boiling water and chill. Cut into halves and scoop out as much flesh as possible, leaving enough skin to hold together.
- In small saucepan, warm butter, sour cream, salt and pepper, then pour contents over potatoes.
- Roast the jalapenos unit black on all sides, place in Ziploc bad and allow to sweat for 10 mins. Scrape off black skins with the back edge of knife blade and remove seeds and stem. Chop peppers and combine with potatoes and add the scallions.
- Mix well and stuff into potato skins. Top each one with grated cheese, pieces of bacon and bake in oven at 325 degrees until warmed through (8-10 mins).

- For extra garnish, top with thinly shaved slices of fresh jalapeno.

21. Smoked Bacon Cheddar Twice Baked Potatoes Recipe

Serving: 14 | Prep: | Cook: 85mins | Ready in:

Ingredients

- 14 medium potatoes, washed and dried
- 1/4 cup butter, melted
- 1 cup shredded sharp cheddar cheese
- pinch of nutmeg
- salt and pepper, to taste
- 4 slices smoked bacon
- 1/4 cup reduced fat milk
- 1/4 cup chives, chopped

Direction

- Preheat oven to 4oo.
- Wrap potatoes in foil, poke each potatoes 3 times on each side with knife to vent.
- Place potatoes on 2 baking sheets and bake until potatoes are soft, about 60 to 70 minutes.
- Remove from oven and let cool.
- Reduce heat to 325.
- While potatoes cook, place bacon in skillet, cook bacon over medium heat until crispy. Drain on paper towel, let cool and crumble bacon.
- Unwrap potatoes, starting on top and 1/2" from each side of potato, use sm. knife to cut out an oval shape along the length of each potato, without breaking the potato skin, scoop out and reserve inside portion of each potato leaving at least a 1/4" wall remaining on the inside, reserve the potato shells.
- Place the reserved inside portion of potatoes in a med. bowl and mash with a fork. Stir in butter, milk, cheese, chives and nutmeg, mix until well combined and season with salt and pepper.

- Place reserved potato shells onto the 2 baking sheets and spoon the potato mixture into each potato shell, top with crumbled bacon.
- Bake potatoes for 10 to 2 minutes or until heated through.

22. Southern Twice Baked Potatoes Recipe

Serving: 6 | Prep: | Cook: 30mins | Ready in:

Ingredients

- 3 large baking potatoes (baked)
- 1/2 stick real butter
- 1/2 cup sour cream
- 1/2 c.diced sweet onion
- 1/2 c. diced green pepper
- salt & pepper to taste
- 1/2 t. garlic powder
- 1/2 c. cream
- 1 c. shredded sharp cheddar cheeze
- 1/3 c.real bacon bits

Direction

- Cut potatoes in half & scoop out middle.
- Combine all ingredients & mix with mixer.
- Re-stuff potatoes in skin & top with additional cheddar cheese
- Optional: sometimes I cook real bacon medium & put slices on top of each potato
- Bake 350 for about 30 minutes

23. Southwest Stuffed Twice Baked Spuds Recipe

Serving: 4 | Prep: | Cook: | Ready in:

Ingredients

- 2 large baking potatoes, rinsed

- 1/2 yellow onion, diced
- 4 cloves of garlic, diced
- 2/3 cup of black beans, soaked and rinsed
- Kale, collards, or swiss chard, rinsed, chopped, ribs removed
- Red bell pepper, deveined and chopped
- 1 cup of shredded cheese, plus 1/2 cup separated for topping (I used 4 cheese Mexican blend)
- Juice from 1 lime
- 3 Tbsp butter
- 1/4 cup Milk
- 1 Tbsp Adobo seasoning
- 2 Tbsp spicy paprika
- A ginormous fistful of cilantro, rinsed and chopped
- 1/4 cup jalapeños, chopped, optional
- You can add chopped tomato, tomatillo, salsa or Pico de Gallo to yours if you wish, I can't have tomato, though I miss it very much.

Direction

- Preheat oven to 400°F.
- Bake potatoes on a baking sheet until soft, about an hour. Let them cool until you're able to safely handle them, about 30 mins.
- During this time, if desired, you may lightly sauté the chopped onions and garlic in a pan with some oil or extra butter, just until fragrant, about 3-4 mins.
- When potatoes are cool, cut them both in half lengthwise, scoop out the majority of the potato flesh into a bowl, leaving a thin layer as a boat to put the stuffing in.
- Add butter, mix until melted. Then add all the other ingredients and blend well. Save some of the shredded cheese, chopped cilantro, and lime juice for the topping.
- Place the filled potatoes back onto the baking sheet, sprinkle the remaining cheese, lime juice, and cilantro now, just to make the tops look good.
- Bake at 400°F for an additional 20-25 mins until cheese is melted and slightly golden.
- Remove and enjoy.

24. Spicy Chili Stuffed Twice Baked Potatoes Recipe

Serving: 2 | Prep: | Cook: 30mins | Ready in:

Ingredients

- 2 Large baking potatoes.
- 1 tsp white pepper.
- 1 tsp hot chili powder.
- 1 heaping tsp cumin.
- 1 heaping tsp oregano.
- 2 TBSP sour cream.
- 1 tsp rainbow colored peppercorns freshly ground.
- 1 TBSP butter or less to your tatse (for those who are watching their weight LOL).
- sea salt to taste.
- 4 strips of bacon diced fine cooked until crisp the crisper the better.
- Enough chili to fill the potato boats 1/2 full.
- Enough shredded habanero cheese or your favorite cheese to cover the top of the potato.

Direction

- Bake potatoes until cooked through cut in half let cool then scrape out leaving enough potato to keep the skin firm.
- Put the potato scrapings in a medium bowl add all the spices, sour cream, bacon mix well.
- Fill the potato boats 1/2 way with the chili.
- Top it off with the potato mixture.
- Bake at 350 degrees for 5 to 10 minutes.
- Turn on the broiler.
- Top with the habanero cheese.
- Put under the broiler and melt the cheese keep a close eye on them so the cheese doesn't burn.
- Serve with cheese covered broccoli.
- Get ready for the spiciest taters you have ever had.

25. Stuffed Baked Potatoes Recipe

Serving: 0 | Prep: | Cook: 45mins | Ready in:

Ingredients

- 3 large baking potatoes, cooked (either bake in oven or microwave)
- 1/4-1/2 cup softened butter
- 1/2 cup sour cream
- 1/4 cup milk
- 1 cup or more shredded cheddar cheese, divided
- 1 tsp seasoning salt
- 1 tsp pepper
- 1 tbsp chives

Direction

- Scoop out the potato pulp and place in large bowl.
- Add rest of ingredients (saving a little cheese for the top of potatoes). Mash altogether.
- Sprinkle with remaining cheese and drizzle a little melted butter on each potato.
- Place on cookie sheet and bake at 350 for 1/2 hour.
- Can be stuffed ahead of time, might need to bake longer!

26. TWICE BAKED POTATOES Recipe

Serving: 10 | Prep: | Cook: 45mins | Ready in:

Ingredients

- 7 cups mashed potatoes (see note)
- one 8 ounce package cream cheese, softened
- one 8 ounce container sour cream
- garlic powder, to taste
- onion powder, to taste
- 1/2 cup (1 stick) butter, melted

Direction

- Heat oven to 350 degrees. In a large mixing bowl, beat together potatoes, cream cheese, and sour cream. Add garlic powder and onion powder and mix well. Place mixture in a glass 13X9 baking dish (or baking dish of similar size). Drizzle melted butter over top. Bake, uncovered, 45-60 mins. Serve hot.
- Note: I was stunned when my neighbour served these for the first time and I found out she had made them with instant mashed potatoes. No one in our family likes instant mashed potatoes because of their funny artificial flavour, but these didn't taste like instant at all! We prefer "real" potatoes, so that is what I use. Recipe is easily halved.

27. TWICE BAKED YUKON GOLD POTATO WITH GOAT CHEESE And Rosemary Recipe

Serving: 6 | Prep: | Cook: 75mins | Ready in:

Ingredients

- 1 1/2 teaspoons vegetable oil
- Eight 6 to 8-ounce yukon gold potatoes, scrubbed and dried
- 5 1/2 ounces soft fresh goat cheese (such as Montrachet), crumbled
- ½ cup buttermilk
- 1 teaspoon fresh rosemary chopped
- 3 tablespoons unsalted butter room temperature
- 3 tablespoons chopped fresh chives
- *Optional ¼ cup fresh beacon bits

Direction

- Position rack in centre of oven; preheat to 375°F. Rub oil over potatoes. Place directly on oven rack; bake until very tender, about 45 minutes. Transfer to rack; cool 10 minutes. Using oven mitts, grasp 1 potato in hand; cut potatoes in half, using spoon, scoop out potato, leaving 1/4-inch-thick shell Repeat with remaining potatoes. Transfer potato flesh to large bowl. Place potato shells back on baking sheet and return hot oven while preparing filling so they will give a nice crispy shell.

- Mash potatoes until smooth. Mix in cheese, then Buttermilk, butter, and chives, Fresh rosemary and Beacon Bits if desired, season with salt and pepper to taste.
- Spoon about 3/4 of potato mixture into shells, dividing evenly. Transfer remaining potato filling to pastry bag fitted with large star tip. Pipe filling atop potatoes; place potatoes on baking sheet.
- Position rack in centre of oven and preheat to 375°F. Bake potatoes until filling is heated through and tops brown, about 20 minutes.

28. Tuna Stuffed Twice Baked Potato Recipe

Serving: 4 | Prep: | Cook: 75mins | Ready in:

Ingredients

- 4 large potatos
- 2 cans tuna, drained and flaked
- 1 can Campbell's cheddar cheese soup
- 8 - 10 medium size mushrooms, chopped in small to mid-size pieces.
- 2 slices Kraft American cheese
- 1/4 cup - 1/2 cup milk (as needed)

Direction

- Bake potato in 375 degree oven for approx. 1 hr. until done. Let cool for about 10 minutes. Slice off top of potato, about a 1/4 inch from the top (lengthwise) and scoop out inside of potato leaving a 1/4 inch or so shell.
- Place scooped out potato in a large bowl, add both cans of tuna, the Campbell's Cheddar Cheese Soup and the sliced mushrooms. Use whatever amount of milk you need to help make mixture smoother although it will be on the chunky side because of the lumps of potato.
- Mix all ingredients and then spoon back into potato shells, mounding high. Place 1/2 slice of American cheese on top.
- Place potatoes back in oven for 15 minutes.
- Remove, let cool for 5-10 minutes then serve.

29. Twice Baked Potato Recipe

Serving: 8 | Prep: | Cook: 75mins | Ready in:

Ingredients

- 4 medium russet potatoes rubbed lightly with olive oil
- 4 ounces sharp cheddar cheese.
- 1/2 cup sour cream
- 1/2 cup buttermilk
- 2 tablespoons unsalted buter
- 4 scallions, sliced
- 1 teaspoon fresh dill
- 1/2 teaspoon sea salt
- fresh ground black pepper

Direction

- Preheat oven to 400 degrees
- Bake potatoes on a baking sheet lined with foil for easy clean up.
- Bake until the skin is a deep brown and a skewer easily pierces the flesh. About 60 minutes.
- Remove potatoes to a wire rack and let cool for ten minutes.
- Slice each potato in half and scoop out the flesh with a spoon, leaving about 1/4 inch of flesh on each shell.
- Return the shells onto the baking sheet and place back into the oven, bake until shells are crisp

- I like to press the flesh through a potato ricer before adding the rest of the ingredients and combine well
- Mound the filling into each potato shell and shape with a fork.
- Place under the broiler until they start to brown and crisp about 10 more minutes
- Allow to cool for a few minutes and serve warm.

30. Twice Baked Potatoes Recipe

Serving: 8 | Prep: | Cook: 120mins | Ready in:

Ingredients

- 4 medium to large baking potatoes
- butter
- 1 cup sour cream
- salt and pepper (to taste)
- garlic powder (to taste)
- bacon bits (optional)
- parsley or green onion (finely chopped)
- 2 cups Shredded cheddar cheese (leave 3/4 cup in reserve)
- 1/4 cup olive oil
- sea salt

Direction

- Preheat oven to 350 degrees
- Prepare potatoes to bake by rubbing them in olive oil
- Stabbing a fork into the potatoes in each end
- Sprinkle sea salt over the oil to stick to the potatoes
- Wrap in foil and bake for one hour
- Take potatoes out of oven and allow them to cool
- When cooled, cut in half, length wise and scoop out potatoes into large bowl
- Place potatoes skins back in oven without foil to harden up some
- Mix all the other ingredients in with the scooped out potatoes and

- Mix well with mixer until smooth and creamy.
- Take hardened skins out of oven and scoop mixture into each one.
- Sprinkle with reserved cheese on top of each and bake again for about 15 to 20 minutes.

31. Twice Baked Potatoes In A Slow Cooker Recipe

Serving: 2 | Prep: | Cook: 300mins | Ready in:

Ingredients

- 2 Large potatoes, washed
- Tin Foil
- 1 cup sour cream
- 1/2 cup milk
- 4 tablespoons butter
- 1 1/2 cup shredded cheddar cheese, divided
- Dash of garlic powder
- Dash of paprika
- salt and pepper to taste
- (Optional)
- Crumbled bacon
- Chopped green onions

Direction

- Find two good sized potatoes and wash them thoroughly. Wrap the potatoes in tin foil and place them in the slow cooker on low for 5-6 hours.
- Once the potatoes are done, carefully slice them in half and scoop out the insides, leaving the skin intact with a bit of potato still attached.
- Place potato innards into a bowl with 1 cup of cheese, the seasoning, milk, butter and sour cream. Mix well.
- Place mixture back inside of potato skin. Garnish with cheese. Add bacon and chopped green onions if desired.
- Place filled potato skins back in the slow cooker on top of tin foil for another hour, or

until cheese is melted and the potato is heated through.

32. Twice Baked Potatoes With Alouette Cheese Recipe

Serving: 4 | Prep: | Cook: 15mins | Ready in:

Ingredients

- 2 medium baking potatoes
- 1 egg
- pinch of nutmeg
- ½ tsp. chopped chives
- ½ cup Alouette Light garlic & herbs Spreadable cheese
- 4 tsp. real bacon pieces, if desired*
- 1 green onion, thinly sliced, if desired

Direction

- Scrub and dry potatoes. Pierce with fork. Microwave on high for 8 to 10 minutes or until soft. Or bake at
- 350° F for 1 hour or until soft.
- Cut potatoes in half. Scoop out flesh into medium bowl, leaving ¼ inch around edge of potato.
- Mash with fork, or mix with a hand held mixer adding the egg, nutmeg, chives and Alouette until well mixed.
- Spoon back into potato shells. Top with bacon.
- Place on microwave-safe dish and microwave on high for 1 to 2 minutes or until thoroughly heated. Or place on oven-safe dish and bake 15 minutes at 350° F or until thoroughly heated.
- Sprinkle with green onion.
- *Look for real bacon pieces in the aisle with the salad dressings. Or you could fry 1 to 2 strips of bacon very crisp, drain and crumble.

33. Twice Baked Potatoes With Broccoli Recipe

Serving: 2 | Prep: | Cook: 80mins | Ready in:

Ingredients

- 2 Baked potatoes
- 2 Tbsp butter
- 2 Tbsp sour cream
- 1/2 Tsp salt
- 2 Tbsp milk
- 1/2 Cup broccoli, cooked and chopped
- 1/4 Cup cheddar cheese

Direction

- Preheat oven to 400 degrees. Bake potatoes for 1 hour.
- Remove potatoes from the oven and let cool for 10 minutes.
- Cut in half and scoop out potato flesh, leaving the skin intact.
- Mash the potato flesh with the butter, sour cream, salt and milk. Fold in the broccoli and cheddar cheese.
- Refill the potato skins with the mixture.
- Place potatoes on a cookie sheet and bake for 10 minutes.
- Serve.

34. Twice Baked Potatoes With Chili And Cheese Recipe

Serving: 4 | Prep: | Cook: 75mins | Ready in:

Ingredients

- 4 baking potatoes
- extra-virgin olive oil
- kosher salt
- 4 tablespoons butter
- 1/4 cup milk
- 1/4 cup sour cream

- 1 1/2 cups shredded cheddar cheese, plus more for topping
- 1 green onion, sliced (or 2 tablespoons chopped chives)
- salt and pepper, to taste
- chili

Direction

- Preheat oven to 400 degrees F. Scrub the potatoes, rub them with olive oil, and pat on kosher salt. Place potatoes on baking sheet, and bake for 1 hour. Set aside until cool enough to handle, about 10 minutes. Lower the oven temperature to 350 degrees F.
- Split potatoes, and scoop most of the flesh into a medium-sized bowl. Add butter, milk, sour cream and cheese. Mash with a potato masher or a fork. Fold in chives, and season with salt and pepper.
- Scoop filling back into potatoes. Top with cheese. Bake for 15 minutes.
- In the meantime, warm the chili in a saucepan over medium heat.
- Garnish potato with chili and cheese before serving.

35. Twice Baked Ranch Potatoes Recipe

Serving: 4 | Prep: | Cook: 80mins | Ready in:

Ingredients

- 4 baking potatoes
- 1/2 cup ranch dressing
- 1/4 cup sour cream
- 1 tablespoon real bacon bits
- 1/4 pound Velveeta cheese cut up

Direction

- Bake potatoes at 400 for 1 hour then slice off tops of potatoes and scoop out.
- Mash potatoes then add dressing, sour cream and bacon bits and beat until fluffy.
- Stir Velveeta into potato mixture then spoon into shells and bake at 350 for 20 minutes.

36. Twice Baked Red Potatoes With Roasted Jalapeno Recipe

Serving: 8 | Prep: | Cook: 40mins | Ready in:

Ingredients

- 5 pounds baby red potatoes
- 2 fresh jalapeno peppers
- 3 T. butter
- 1/2 c. sour cream
- 3 strips bacon, cooked & chopped
- 1/2 t. salt
- 1/2 t. freshly ground black pepper
- 3 chopped scallions, green parts only
- 1/2 C. grated cheddar cheese

Direction

- Boil the potatoes in water for 15 minutes. Remove the potatoes and set aside for 10 minutes. Slice potatoes in half and scoop the flesh into a large bowl; save skin boats. In a saucepan, warm the butter, sour cream, salt and pepper. Add the warmed mixture to the potato flesh and set aside. Roast the jalapenos until the skin is black on all sides, then place in a Ziploc bag to rest for 10 minutes so the skin fully lifts off the pepper. Peel off the black skins and remove the seeds and stem. Chop the roasted jalapenos and scallions and combine with the potato flesh. Spoon or use a Ziploc bag with hole cut into corner to pipe filling into shells. Top each with grated cheese & bacon and bake in the oven at 325 degrees F. for 10 minutes. Garnish with thin slices of jalapeno.

37. Twice Baked Sweet Potatoes Recipe

Serving: 4 | Prep: | Cook: 75mins | Ready in:

Ingredients

- 6 sweet potatoes, even in size and scrubbed
- 4 tablespoons brown sugar
- 4 tablespoons butter, room temperature
- 4 ounces cream cheese, room temperature
- 1/2 teaspoon ground cinnamon
- 1/4 teaspoon ground nutmeg
- 1/4 teaspoon ground ginger
- salt and freshly ground black pepper

Direction

- Preheat oven to 375 degrees F.
- Place sweet potatoes on sheet tray and bake for 1 hour or until soft.
- Remove from oven and let stand until cool enough to handle.
- Split potatoes and remove the flesh to a medium sized bowl, reserving skins.
- In another bowl, add brown sugar, butter and cream cheese and the all of the spices and mash with a fork or rubber spatula.
- Add the butter and cream cheese mixture to the sweet potato flesh and fold in completely.
- Add the filling back to the potato skins and place on a half sheet tray.
- Bake for 15 minutes or until golden brown.

38. Twice Baked Sweet Potatoes With A Flare" Recipe

Serving: 6 | Prep: | Cook: 8mins | Ready in:

Ingredients

- 6 sweet potatoes, even in size and scrubbed
- 4 tablespoons brown sugar
- 4 tablespoons butter, room temperature
- 4 ounces cream cheese, room temperature
- 1/2 teaspoon ground cinnamon
- 1/4 teaspoon ground nutmeg
- 1/4 teaspoon ground ginger
- 2cups mini marshmallows
- salt and freshly ground black pepper
- 1/4 cup Coarse chopped pecans for topping
- Pure cane sugar and cinnamon for garnish sprinkle

Direction

- Preheat oven to 375 degrees F.
- Place sweet potatoes on sheet tray and bake for 1 hour or until soft. Remove from oven and let stand until cool enough to handle.
- Split potatoes and remove the flesh to a medium sized bowl, reserving skins. In another bowl, add brown sugar, butter and cream cheese and the all of the spices and mash with a fork or rubber spatula.
- Add the butter and cream cheese mixture to the sweet potato flesh and fold in completely. Add the filling back to the potato skins and place on a half sheet tray. Bake for 10 minutes add mini marshmallows along with some pecans place back into oven for 5 minutes or until golden brown.
- Garnish with a sprinkle of cinnamon and sugar mixture
- Let cool for 5 minutes or so.
- Enjoy every bite :)

39. Twice Baked White Cheddar Sage Potatoes Recipe

Serving: 20 | Prep: | Cook: 45mins | Ready in:

Ingredients

- 10 russet potatoes, relatively same size
- 1 lb white cheddar, strip grated
- 1 pint heavy cream, hot
- 3 tbsp unsalted butter
- 1/4 c sage minced
- salt and pepper to taste

Direction

- Place each potato in oven at 350 degrees for 30 minutes or until yielding depending on oven and size of potato. Do not poke holes in them you need the skin intact.
- Cut each potato in half lengthwise and scoop as much of the meat out without damaging skin.
- Lay the hollowed skins on a sheet tray and the innards into a stand mixer bowl.
- Add the cream, butter, sage, 10 oz. of the white cheddar to the potato and mix with the paddle.
- Taste it and add salt and pepper. Or more butter depending on your potato size.
- Do not overwork the potatoes when they are creamy stop!
- Transfer the mixture to a piping bag or Ziploc bag and pipe into the individual skins. Just enough to level.
- Even out any gaps in the potatoes.
- Cover each potato with the remaining cheddar.
- This is when you can hold them for up to a day.
- When ready place them in a 375 degree oven until melted. Then use the broiler to make them golden. Switching to the broiler will help the potatoes say moist.

40. Twice Baked Yams Recipe

Serving: 6 | Prep: | Cook: 30mins | Ready in:

Ingredients

- 3 medium yams
- 3 teaspoons vegetable oil
- 2 tablespoons butter
- 2 tablespoons brown sugar
- 1/4 cup raisins
- 1/4 cup finely chopped pecans
- 3 tablespoons crushed pineapple drained
- 1/2 teaspoon cinnamon
- miniature marshmallows

Direction

- Wash potatoes then blot dry and prick with a fork to allow steam to escape.
- Rub a light coating of vegetable oil onto skins.
- Bake at 375 for 45 minutes.
- Cut a thin lengthwise slice from top of each potato.
- Scoop out inside being careful to leave a thin shell.
- Mash potatoes in a mixing bowl until no lumps remain.
- Add butter, brown sugar, raisins, nuts, drained pineapple and cinnamon.
- Fill potato skins with mixture.
- Increase oven to 400.
- Place potatoes in an oven proof dish and bake for 20 minutes.
- Remove dish from oven then set oven to broil.
- Place several miniature marshmallows on top of each potato then place under broiler.

41. Twice Smashed Baked Potatoes Recipe

Serving: 4 | Prep: | Cook: 80mins | Ready in:

Ingredients

- 4 large russet potatoes, each about 3/4 pound each, well scrubbed
- 1/2 pound broccoli florets, blanched
- 4 tablespoons softened butter
- 1/2 cup sour cream
- 1/2 cup shredded sharp Cheddar, plus extra for topping
- 1/2 cup shredded smoked Gouda, plus extra for topping
- salt and freshly ground black pepper
- butter, for serving, optional

Direction

- Preheat the oven to 400 degrees F.
- Pierce potatoes with fork. Place on centre rack of oven and cook for 1 hour.
- Remove from oven and let cool slightly. Using a paring knife, cut a canoe-like top out of the potatoes. Scoop the flesh into a large mixing bowl, leaving a 1/2-inch thick wall around the skin.
- Add the blanched broccoli to the potatoes. Stir in the butter, sour cream, Cheddar, Gouda, and salt and pepper; and mash until creamy.
- Using a small spoon, scoop the filling back into the potatoes. It will be a nice mounded pile of filling. Sprinkle with more of both cheeses on top of the potatoes.
- Set the potatoes on a baking sheet and bake for 15 to 20 minutes, until heated through and cheese is melted and gooey. Serve with butter, if desired.

42. Twice Baked Potato Chicken Pot Pie Recipe

Serving: 1 | Prep: | Cook: 60mins | Ready in:

Ingredients

- Twice Baked potato chicken pot pie
- Large baking potato
- chicken ala king or your own chicken pot pie ingredients
- salt
- pepper
- (this is my own ingredients for the pot pie ingredients. 2 (10 oz) cans Campbell's Cream of Chicken Soup or
- Campbell's chicken or turkey Pot Pie Soup
- 2 (about 9 oz) packages frozen mixed vegetables, thawed
- 2 cups cubed, cooked chicken
- 1 cup chicken broth combined with 2 tablespoons flour) This should be enough filling for several potatoes.

Direction

- Directions
- Bake potato till done. Remove from oven and lay on side
- Cut big enough hole in potato so you can scoop out the inside.
- Fill the potato with your favorite pot pie mix and cover hole in potato with the some of the potato that you scooped out
- . Bake at 400 degrees till top turns brown.
- Eat skin and all.

43. Twice Baked Potatoes Recipe

Serving: 8 | Prep: | Cook: 70mins | Ready in:

Ingredients

- 8 baking potatoes
- 16 oz sour cream
- 1 tbls butter
- 1/4 c milk
- 1 c cheese divided in half
- 1 tsp garlic
- 1/4 c real bacon pieces
- 2 tbls chives

Direction

- Wash potatoes and wrap in aluminum foil
- Bake in oven 1 hour at 350 degrees
- Once potatoes are tender slice lengthwise in half
- Scoop out the centre and keep the skins
- Put the centre in a large mixing bowl
- Using a mixer beat in all ingredients except for half the cheese and half the chives until blended
- Put mixture back into the skins
- Top with remaining cheese and chives and bake in oven 10 mins or until the cheese melts

44. Twice Baked Mashed Potatoes Recipe

Serving: 10 | Prep: | Cook: 30mins | Ready in:

Ingredients

- 1 (22 oz) package frozen Ora-Ida mashed potatoes
- 1/2 (8 oz) cream cheese, softened
- 1/2 cup sour cream
- 1/4 cup chopped fresh chives
- 4 bacon slices, cooked and crumbled
- 1/2 teaspoon seasoned pepper
- 1/4 teaspoon salt
- 1/2 cup (2oz) shredded cheddar cheese

Direction

- Prepare potatoes according to package directions.
- Stir in cream cheese and next five ingredients.
- Put in 6 ramekins or a 2-quart baking dish.
- Sprinkle with cheese.
- Bake at 350 degrees for 20-30 minutes.

45. Twice Baked Potato Skins W Pepperoni Recipe

Serving: 30 | Prep: | Cook: 75mins | Ready in:

Ingredients

- 10 Large (whole) Russet or idaho potatoes, scrubbed
- 2 1/2 to 3 cups of pepperoni, diced
- 1/3 Cup milk
- 1 Cup butter or margarine
- 1/2 tspn cayenne pepper
- 2 tbspns oregano
- 3 tbspns garlic powder
- salt, black pepper to taste
- parsley or chives to Garnish

Direction

- Preheat oven to 400F. Arrange potatoes in a large baking pan and bake for 1 hour, or until potatoes are soft.
- In the meantime, if you haven't already, dice the pepperoni.
- Remove from oven, but leave the heat on because you'll be putting them back in soon.
- Cut each potato into 3 wedges, scooping out only half of the potato into a large mixing bowl, leaving a decent layer of potato above the skin so it holds its basic shape.
- When you've gathered all the potato flesh into the bowl, add butter, milk, salt, Pepper, Garlic, Oregano and Cayenne.
- Mash with potato masher until smooth.
- Pile the mashed potatoes evenly back into the potato skins, arranging them back into the baking pan in a single layer. (No laying them on top of each other!) You may need an extra pan for this.
- Arrange the pepperoni evenly on top of the potato skins, then sprinkle either the Parsley or Chives to garnish the tops. (I add Parsley and extra Garlic)
- Bake for an additional 15 minutes, then remove, arrange on plate and enjoy.
- You may also add black olives, cheddar and/or Monterey Jack cheese, onions, etc. The options are limitless!

46. Twice Baked Stuffed Potatoes Recipe

Serving: 2 | Prep: | Cook: 10mins | Ready in:

Ingredients

- 2 baking potatoes
- 1/2 cup (or more) sour cream - I don't measure something like this!
- 1/2 cup (or more) shredded cheddar - "
- Minced garlic (optional, sometimes I do, sometimes I don't)

- Chopped green onions or chives (usually use, but didn't have any last night)
- salt and pepper to taste
- THAT'S IT!

Direction

- Cut a slit around very top portion on each potato in a circle till it meets the other side
- Place in microwave oven (you can bake in a conventional oven, but WHY in this heat)
- Ovens vary, mine has a sensor cook with a baked potato setting I just hit for 2 potatoes
- When done, let cool so you can touch them, lift off "lid" and (I use a grapefruit spoon) scoop out potato innards being careful not to get too close to skin so that it doesn't tear.
- Put innards in bowl and mash up adding sour cream, cheese and onions and garlic if using.
- Stuff back into potato skins - there will be a lot more stuffing that before
- Put back in micro just before your meat is ready and nuke a couple minutes if necessary to reheat - I say this because you can make them ahead of time by quite a while.

47. Twice Baked Buttermilk Potatoes Recipe

Serving: 4 | Prep: | Cook: 15mins | Ready in:

Ingredients

- 3 large russet potatoes
- 1 tbsp butter or Earth Balance
- 3/4 cup buttermilk
- sea salt and freshly ground black pepper, to taste
- 1/2 cup shredded white cheddar
- olive oil spray (regular cooking spray is OK too)
- 1/4 cup grated Parmesan

Direction

- Bake potatoes in 350F oven until tender but still firm.
- Remove from oven and allow to cool enough to handle.
- Cut each potato in half. Scoop out flesh, leaving a firm 1/4-inch shell on 4 of the halves.
- Mash potatoes in a small bowl. Add butter, buttermilk, and shredded cheddar. Season to taste with salt & pepper.
- Spray inside of each of the 4 potato shells with olive oil and sprinkle with salt & pepper. Fill the shells with mashed potato mixture. They will be heaping. Divide grated Parmesan over tops of each potato.
- Bake at 350F for 15-20 minutes or until heated through.
- If tops haven't browned much, place potatoes under the broiler for 2-4 minutes. Be sure to check on them so they don't burn.

48. Twice Baked Spinach Potatoes Recipe

Serving: 2 | Prep: | Cook: 2hours | Ready in:

Ingredients

- 2 large baking potatoes, washed
- 1/2 cup grated cheddar cheese
- 1 cup packed fresh spinach, chopped
- margarine
- evaporated milk

Direction

- Prick the potatoes with a fork a couple of times and bake them in a 350F oven for one hour.
- Remove from oven and slice the top of the potato off horizontally so that you open up the main potato below almost like a boat.
- Gently remove the potato pulp from the top of the potato you've just removed and gently scoop out the potato pulp from the rest of the potato as well. Leave a bit left in just to help

- add rigidity to the shell and you don't want to make a hole in the potato where it would leak!
- Now in a bowl mash the potato pulp up with margarine and evaporated milk or whatever it is you like to mash potatoes with.
- Add the cheddar cheese and spinach to the potato mixture and mix well.
- Now scoop up all that yummy, spinach potato mixture and put it back into the potato shell.
- Bake for another 40 minutes until the potato is nice and hot and crispy golden brown on the top!
- Enjoy!

49. Twiced Baked New Potatoes Recipe

Serving: 20 | Prep: | Cook: 30mins | Ready in:

Ingredients

- 1-1/2 pounds small new potatoes
- 2 teaspoons sea salt
- 1 teaspoon coarsely black pepper
- 3 tablespoons vegetable oil
- 1/2 cup shredded monterrey jack cheese
- 1/2 cup shredded asiago cheese
- 1/2 cup sour cream
- 3 ounces cream cheese
- 1/3 cup minced green onions
- 1 teaspoon basil
- 1 clove minced garlic
- 1 teaspoon salt
- 2 teaspoons freshly ground black pepper
- 1 pound bacon
- 1 package dry ranch dressing

Direction

- Preheat oven to 400.
- Pierce potatoes with fork several times and rub with oil.
- Combine salt and pepper together and roll boiled potatoes in this mixture before baking.
- Place in single layer in non-stick cooking sprayed shallow baking pan.
- Bake uncovered for 50 minutes and allow to cool.
- Combine cheeses, sour cream, green onions, basil, garlic, salt, pepper, 1/2 of bacon and dressing.
- Mix well.
- When potatoes are cool enough to handle cut in half and scoop out pulp from middle of potatoes.
- Add to cheese mixture and mix until all ingredients are well blended.
- Stuff mixture back into potatoes then top with remaining bacon.
- Bake an additional 15 minutes.

50. Ultimate Twice Baked Potatoes Recipe

Serving: 8 | Prep: | Cook: 75mins | Ready in:

Ingredients

- 4 large baking potatoes
- 8 slices bacon
- 1 cup sour cream
- 1/2 cup milk
- 4 tablespoons butter
- 1/2 teaspoon salt
- 1/2 teaspoon pepper
- 1 cup shredded cheddar cheese, divided
- 8 green onions, sliced, divided

Direction

- Preheat oven to 350 degrees F (175 degrees C).
- Bake potatoes in preheated oven for 1 hour.
- Meanwhile, place bacon in a large, deep skillet. Cook over medium high heat until evenly brown. Drain, crumble and set aside.
- When potatoes are done allow them to cool for 10 minutes. Slice potatoes in half lengthwise and scoop the flesh into a large bowl; save skins. To the potato flesh add sour cream,

milk, butter, salt, pepper, 1/2 cup cheese and 1/2 the green onions. Mix with a hand mixer until well blended and creamy. Spoon the mixture into the potato skins. Top each with remaining cheese, green onions and bacon.
- Bake for another 15 minutes.

51. Veggie Marscapone Twice Baked Potatoes Recipe

Serving: 2 | Prep: | Cook: 55mins | Ready in:

Ingredients

- 2 large potatoes scrubbed and salted lightly
- 2 large broccoli spears steamed and florets removed
- 2 level tbls sour cream. room temp.
- 1 pat butter
- 1 clove garlic
- 2-3 tbls marscapone at room temp.
- kosher salt and white pepper to taste
- 1 tbls grated mozzarella, room temp
- fresh chopped parsel y
- paprika
- optional finely chopped hot red pepper, cooked and seeds removed

Direction

- Bake potatoes in oven
- Cut baked potatoes in half when cooled
- In a bowl scoop out potatoes leaving about 1/8-1/4 inch on skin
- Add sour cream, butter, mascarpone, pressed garlic, and lightly mashed broccoli florets (hot pepper optional)
- Gently stir and fluff
- Fill potatoes
- Sprinkle mozzarella, parsley and paprika on top
- Heat slowly in 250-300 oven until cheese is melted.
- Under broiler for 1 minute to brown

52. Veggie Twice Baked Potatoes Recipe

Serving: 8 | Prep: | Cook: 120mins | Ready in:

Ingredients

- 4 large baking potatoes - baked
- 2 Tb olive oil
- 1/2 green pepper - chopped
- 2 cloves garlic- chopped
- 1/2 cup sliced mushrooms- chopped
- 1 Tb fresh parsley - chopped
- 3Tb butter
- 3/4 cup milk
- 1 cup shredded cheddar cheese - divided in half
- salt and pepper to tast

Direction

- Preheat oven to 450
- Bake potatoes until done approx. 1 1/2 hours
- Preheat the oil in a small skillet and sauté' the garlic, green pepper, parsley and mushroom until soft
- Remove potatoes and spoon out the insides reserving the skins
- Combine potatoes, butter, milk and 1/2 of the cheddar - mash
- Add garlic pepper mushrooms and mix.
- Fill the reserved skins with the mashed potatoes top with cheese and bake an additional 20 mins until cheese is melted.

53. Yams Twice Baked Recipe

Serving: 6 | Prep: | Cook: 30mins | Ready in:

Ingredients

- 3 medium yams
- vegetable oil

- 2 tablespoons butter
- 2 tablespoons brown sugar
- 1/4 cup raisins
- 1/4 cup finely chopped pecans
- 3 tablespoons crushed pineapple drained
- 1/2 teaspoon cinnamon
- miniature marshmallows

Direction

- Wash potatoes then blot dry and prick with a fork to allow steam to escape.
- Rub a light coating of vegetable oil onto potato skins then bake at 375 for 45 minutes.
- Cut a thin lengthwise slice from the top of each potato.
- Scoop out inside being careful to leave a thin shell.
- Mash potatoes in a mixing bowl until no lumps remain.
- Add butter, brown sugar, raisins, nuts, drained pineapple and cinnamon.
- Fill potato skins with mixture.
- Increase oven to 400 and place potatoes in an oven proof dish and bake for 20 minutes.
- Remove dish from oven then set oven to broil.
- Place several marshmallows on top of each potato then place under broiler for 5 minutes.

54. Twice Baked Onion Potatoes Recipe

Serving: 8 | Prep: | Cook: 105mins | Ready in:

Ingredients

- 4 large baking potatoes
- 1 pound of sliced bacon chopped
- 1 to 1 and 1/2 cups finely chopped onion
- 1/2 cup sour cream
- 2 to 3 tablespoons milk
- 1 cup diced American cheese
- 1/2 cup shredded chedder cheese
- 4 green onions finely sliced

Direction

- Preheat oven to 400 degrees
- Bake potatoes for one hour or until tender
- While potatoes are baking cook the bacon in a skillet until crisp
- Remove bacon from skillet to paper towels
- Drain drippings reserving 1 tablespoon
- In drippings sauté onions until tender and set aside
- When potatoes cool enough to handle cut in half lengthwise
- Scoop out pulp leaving about a 1/8 inch shell
- In a bowl beat the potato pulp sour cream and milk until creamy
- Stir in the onions American cheese and 1 cup of the bacon
- Spoon mixture bake into the shells
- Place on a baking sheet and return to the oven for 25 minutes
- Remove from oven and sprinkle on the cheddar cheese remaining bacon and green onion slices
- Return to the oven just until the cheddar cheese is nicely melted

55. Twice Baked Potato Sheet Cake Recipe

Serving: 20 | Prep: | Cook: 30mins | Ready in:

Ingredients

- potato 5 lb bag
- bacon one pound fried crisp and crushed sliced minced -but get it to bacon bits
- onion two fist sized vidalias diced
- grated cheese one pound of colby
- sour cream one cup
- real butter (or dont bother) two sticks sliced to pats
- one handful fresh chives

Direction

- Boil peeled cubed potatoes until tender
- Mash still warm potato's and add sour cream and butter until it's all creamy
- Add raw onions and mix well
- On a tin foil covered sheet cake pan lay out potato mixture covering entire pan (about a half inch thick)
- Sprinkle with crisp bacon chips
- Toss your chives at it lawn like lawn clippings
- Coat with shredded cheese
- Bake for thirty minutes at 350
- Slice into serving sizes of your choosing and serve hot...

56. Twice Baked Potatoes Recipe

Serving: 4 | Prep: | Cook: 15mins | Ready in:

Ingredients

- 2 potatoes, scrubbed and pricked all over with a fork
- 2 T butter
- salt and pepper to taste
- 1/3 c milk
- 1 c cheese (your choice, I usually use cheddar and parm, I used a really good aged Gouda this time and it was awesome), grated
- a little hot sauce

Direction

- Microwave the potatoes, on a paper towel, for about 10 minutes, turning halfway through, until fork-tender.
- Preheat the oven to 350.
- Cut potatoes in half the long way, and scoop out the insides carefully into a bowl, trying not to break up the skin.
- Place the 4 skin boats onto a cookie sheet.
- Mash the potatoes with the rest of the ingredients, then scoop the mix into the skins.
- Sprinkle with a little more cheese if desired, then bake about 20 minutes until beginning to brown.

57. Twice Baked Potatoes Master Recipe Recipe

Serving: 8 | Prep: | Cook: 75mins | Ready in:

Ingredients

- 4 russet potatoes,scrubbed,dried and slightly oiled(can use youkon gold for a flavor change)
- 4 ounces sharp cheddar cheeese,shredded(about 1 cup)-can change cheeses to gruyere,fontina or feta
- 1/2 cup sour cream
- 1/2 cup buttermilk
- 2 Tbs. butter,room temp.
- 3 scallions,white and green parts,thinly sliced.(about t 1/2 cup)1/2 tsp salt
- pepper to taste

Direction

- Adjust oven rack to upper middle and preheat to 400F.
- Place boiled potatoes on a foil covered baking sheet
- Bake for about 1 hour-till skin is deep brown and crisp and skewer easily pierces the flesh
- Transfer potatoes to a wire rack and let cool for 10 minutes
- Cut potatoes in half-length wise and scoop out flesh, leaving about 1/4" inside shell,
- Place shells on sheet pan and return to oven until dry and slightly crisp, about 10 minutes
- Mash potatoes with a fork and add all of the ingredients, combine well
- Remove shells, increase oven temp. To broil, spoon mixture back into the shells and return to oven and broil till spotty brown and crisp.
- >with pepper jack cheese and bacon
- Fry 8 strips of bacon, cut into 1/4" strips till crisp, remove bacon to paper lined plate to drain. Follow main recipe and substituting cheese
- >

- >with Indian spices and peas
- heat 2 Tbs. butter, over medium heat in a skillet, sauté 1 cup finely chopped onion, until soft, add 1 tsp. grated ginger root,3 minced cloves of garlic,1 tsp. each of ground cumin and ground coriander,1/4 tsp. Each of ground cinnamon, ground turmeric and ground cloves, cook till fragrant about 30 seconds, taking care not to brown garlic... off heat stir in 1 cup of thawed frozen peas. Omit cheese and butter. Follow recipe

Chapter 2: Awesome Baked Potato Recipes

***

58. Alpine Potato Bake Recipe

Serving: 8 | Prep: | Cook: 60mins | Ready in:

Ingredients

- 2 lbs. potatoes
- 1 cup chopped onion
- 1/4 cup butter or margarine
- 2 T. all purpose flour
- 1/4 tsp. pepper
- 2 T. spicy brown mustard
- 2 cups chicken broth or bouillion
- 1 tsp. horseradish
- 1/4 cup dried bread crumbs

Direction

- Butter a 2 qt. rectangular baking dish.
- In a 3 qt. saucepan, cook potatoes in boiling salted water until tender.
- Drain and let cool.
- Preheat oven to 375
- In the same saucepan over med. heat, sauté onion in butter for 10 min. or until tender and golden.
- Stir in flour and pepper, then broth.
- Stirring, bring to a boil and boil for 1 min. Remove from heat.
- Whisk in spicy brown mustard and horseradish.
- Slice potatoes 1/2" thick.
- Layer in baking dish.
- Cover potatoes with sauce and sprinkle with bread crumbs.
- Bake for 15-20 minutes or until hot and bubbly.

59. Apple Sweet Potato Bake Recipe

Serving: 6 | Prep: | Cook: 45mins | Ready in:

Ingredients

- 5 cups thinly sliced sweet potatoes (or yams), about 1 1/2 sweet potatoes
- 2 cups thinly sliced apples, such as pippin or Granny Smith (about 2 small)
- 1/4 cup dark brown sugar, packed
- 2 tablespoons reduced-calorie pancake syrup
- 1/2 teaspoon ground cinnamon
- 1/2 cup apple juice or orange juice
- 1/4 cup walnut pieces or chopped walnuts

Direction

- 1. Preheat oven to 375 degrees.
- 2. In a large bowl, toss the sweet potatoes, apple slices, and brown sugar together. Spoon into a 9x9-inch or similar-sized baking dish.
- 3. In a small bowl, blend syrup with cinnamon. Stir in the apple juice. Pour evenly over sweet potato mixture. Sprinkle walnuts over the top.
- 4. Cover baking dish with lid or foil and bake for 30 minutes. Remove foil and bake about 15

minutes longer (or until apple and sweet potatoes are cooked throughout).

60. B Grill Chili Cheese Stuffed Baked Potato Recipe

Serving: 1 | Prep: | Cook: 70mins | Ready in:

Ingredients

- BAKE AS MANY potatoes AS NEEDED
- Nice size baking potatoes
- Crisco
- Favorite meaty chili (home-made is best)
- mild cheddar cheese or your favorite cheese
- sour cream
- Chopped green onions

Direction

- Lightly rub potatoes with Crisco
- Place in a 375 degree oven for about an hour, depending on the size of the potato
- When potato is done, remove from oven
- Cut in half while hot
- Place in an oven proof dish (may use baking sheet for a number of potatoes)
- Top with your favorite chili, then top with cheese
- Return to oven until chili is bubbly and cheese is melted
- Remove from oven
- Place on serving plate
- Serve with sour cream and chopped green onions
- A DELICIOUS SIMPLE MEAL

61. BAKED NEW POTATO SALAD WITH PEANUTS AND MUSTARD Recipe

Serving: 8 | Prep: | Cook: 30mins | Ready in:

Ingredients

- 1/2 cup red peanuts
- 2 pounds small red new potatoes scrubbed
- 2 tablespoon olive oil
- 1/4 teaspoon salt
- Freshly ground black pepper to taste
- 2 tablespoon rice vinegar
- 1/2 cup minced red onion
- 2 large carrot sliced on the diagonal 1/4" thick
- 2 medium ribs celery sliced on the diagonal 1/4" thick
- 1/2 cup mayonnaise
- 1/2 cup plain yogurt
- 2 tablespoons finely chopped cilantro
- 2 tablespoon grainy mustard
- 2 tablespoon Dijon mustard
- 1/2 teaspoon ground cumin

Direction

- Put peanuts in a small baking pan and toast in preheated 350 oven 5 minutes.
- Cool slightly then rub in a kitchen towel to remove skins and chop coarsely.
- Cut potatoes into quarters and place in a baking pan.
- Toss with olive oil, salt and several grindings of pepper.
- Bake in a preheated 375 oven for 30 minutes stirring occasionally.
- Remove from oven then toss with vinegar and cool.
- Place diced red onion in small bowl and cover with ice water.
- Let sit 20 minutes to reduce acidity.
- Drain and squeeze out excess moisture with a paper towel.
- Bring a small pan of water to a boil then add carrots and cook 2 minutes.

- Drain and rinse with cold water to stop the cooking then pat dry.
- Combine the cooled potatoes, onion, carrots and celery in a large bowl.
- Stir together mayonnaise, yogurt, cilantro, mustards, cumin and several grindings black pepper.
- Combine with vegetables and refrigerate then stir in peanuts just before serving.

62. BEER BATTER BAKED POTATOES Recipe

Serving: 4 | Prep: | Cook: 40mins | Ready in:

Ingredients

- 4 lg. baking potatoes
- 1 c. corn flake crumbs
- beer BATTER:
- 1 1/2 c. flour
- 1 can beer
- 1 egg
- salt and pepper

Direction

- Bake potatoes until nearly done. Dip in beer batter, roll in corn flake crumbs. Deep fry until brown. Return to oven (325 degrees F.) and bake until done.
- Beer Batter: Separate egg. Set aside egg white. Blend ingredients with mixer, using only the egg yolk. Let stand for 1 hour. Then beat egg white until stiff and fold into batter. Let stand for 1 hour before using.

63. BEER BAKED SCALLOPED POTATOES Recipe

Serving: 6 | Prep: | Cook: 25mins | Ready in:

Ingredients

- 1 tsp vegetable oil
- 1½ cups vertically sliced onion
- 1 cup beer
- 2 lbs medium red potatoes, peeled and cut into 1/8-inch slices
- ½ tsp salt, divided
- ¼ tsp pepper, divided
- 2 Tbs flour
- ½ cup nonfat milk
- ½ cup (2 ounces) grated swiss cheese

Direction

- 1. Preheat oven to 350°F.
- 2. Coat a large skillet with cooking spray; add oil, and place over medium heat until hot. Add onion, and sauté 5 minutes. Add beer; cook 12 minutes or until liquid evaporates, stirring occasionally. Remove onion mixture from heat, and set aside.
- 3. Cook potato slices in boiling water for 8 minutes or until crisp-tender; drain. Rinse under cold water, and drain well.
- 4. Place one-third of potato slices in an 11×7-inch baking dish coated with cooking spray, and sprinkle with half of salt and half of pepper. Spread half of onion mixture over potato slices. Repeat procedure with the remaining potato slices, salt, pepper and onion mixture, ending with potato slices.
- 5. Place flour in bowl. Gradually add milk, stirring with a wire whisk until blended. Pour milk mixture evenly over potato slices. Cover with aluminum foil, and cut 3 (1-inch) slits in foil. Bake 45 minutes. Uncover; sprinkle with cheese, and bake an additional 10 minutes or until cheese melts.
- Serving Size: 1 cup

64. Baby Bake Potatoes W Bleu Cheese Topping Recipe

Serving: 5 | Prep: | Cook: 45mins | Ready in:

Ingredients

- 20 small new potatoes
- 1/4 cup vegetable oil
- coarse salt
- 1/2 cup sour cream
- 1/4 cup crumbled bleu cheese
- 2 tablespoons chopped fresh chives

Direction

- Preheat oven 350
- Wash/dry potatoes
- Pour oil in bowl
- Add potatoes, toss to coat well
- Dip potatoes in salt to coat lightly
- Spread potatoes on baking sheet, bake until tender 45-50 minutes
- In small bowl combine sour cream and bleu cheese
- Cut a cross on top of each potato. Press with fingertip to open potato.
- Top each with dollop of mixture. Sprinkle with chives.
- ENJOY

65. Bacon Wrapped Potatoes Recipe

Serving: 4 | Prep: | Cook: 60mins | Ready in:

Ingredients

- 8 slices bacon, cut in half crosswise
- 16 small potatoes
- toothpicks

Direction

- Preheat oven to 400.
- Wrap each piece of bacon around a potato and secure with toothpick.
- Place in baking dish and bake till bacon is crisp and potatoes tender when pierced with a fork, 40-50 mins. Leave toothpick in and serve as appetizer or remove and serve as side dish.

66. Bake Sweet Potatoes W African Style Peanut Sauce Recipe

Serving: 6 | Prep: | Cook: 1mins | Ready in:

Ingredients

- 6 medium sweet potatoes (about 3 lbs)
- 1 teaspoon canola oil
- 1/3 finely chopped onion
- 1 tablespoon of fresh grated ginger
- 2 garlic cloves minced
- 1 1/2 teaspoons ground cumin
- 1 1/2 teaspoons ground coriander
- 1/8 of ground red pepper
- 3/4 cup of H20
- 3/4 cup of tomato sauce
- 1/4 cup of peanut butter
- 1 teaspoon of sugar
- 1/4 teaspoon of salt
- 2 tablespoons of chopped fresh cilantro

Direction

- Pre-heat oven to 375
- Pierce potatoes with a fork
- Bake at 375 for an hour or so or until tender
- Cool potatoes slightly
- Heat oil in a medium skillet over medium-low heat Add onion, ginger, and garlic, cook 3 mins. Add cumin, coriander, and pepper, cook 1 min. Add 3/4 cup of H20 and then tomato sauce, PB, sugar and salt! Stirring until smooth, bring to a simmer and Cook 2 mins. Or until thick
- Split potatoes lengthwise, cutting to, but not through, other side, spoon about 1/4 cup

sauce onto each potato with 1 teaspoon of cilantro!

67. Baked Apples With Sweet Potato Stuffing Recipe

Serving: 6 | Prep: | Cook: 20mins | Ready in:

Ingredients

- 6 baking apples-peeled and cored
- 1/2 cup cinnamom red hot candies
- 1 cup water
- 1 (29 ounce) can sweet potatoes, drained
- 1/3 cup packed brown sugar
- 1/2 cup crushed pineapple, drained
- 1/4 cup chopped pecans
- 6 large marshmallows

Direction

- Preheat oven to 350 F.
- In a large pot over medium heat, combine the candies and water. Stir until candies are dissolved. Add the apples and baste frequently until apples begin to soften. Remove from heat and allow to cool.
- Mix together the sweet potatoes, brown sugar, pineapple and pecans. Stuff the cooled apples with the sweet potato mixture. Mound any remaining mixture on top of apples.
- place in 4 quart casserole dish and bake for 20 minutes; place a marshmallow on each apple, return to oven and cook until marshmallows are golden brown.

68. Baked Bacon Wrapped New Potatoes Recipe

Serving: 8 | Prep: | Cook: 45mins | Ready in:

Ingredients

- 8 new potatoes
- butter
- 8 slices of bacon (uncooked)
- cheese
- sour cream
- green onions

Direction

- First preheat oven to 350 degrees.
- Next tear 8 strips of aluminum foil each big enough to cover a new potato.
- Wash the potatoes and poke holes in them with a fork.
- Put a small pat of butter on one of the aluminum sheets. Wrap a slice of bacon around a new potato and place on top of the pat of butter and then wrap the aluminum around the potato covering it completely. Repeat this step for each potato.
- Place the potatoes in the preheated oven on the top shelf with an empty cookie sheet on the bottom shelf to catch any drippings during cooking from the butter and bacon.
- Potatoes are done when you can squeeze them softly with your hand (please use a pot holder when checking potatoes).
- Serve with extra butter, cheese, sour cream and green onions if desired.

69. Baked Carrots And Potatoes Recipe

Serving: 4 | Prep: | Cook: 30mins | Ready in:

Ingredients

- 2 tablespoons butter
- 4 medium baking potatoes sliced
- 4 medium carrots sliced
- 1 medium onion cubed
- 1 teaspoon salt
- 1 teaspoon freshly ground black pepper
- 1/2 teaspoon sweet paprika
- 1/2 cup evaporated milk

- 1/2 cup water

Direction

- Preheat oven to 350.
- Butter a square baking dish.
- Place vegetables in dish and dot with butter.
- Mix seasonings with the milk and water then pour over the vegetables.
- Bake stirring occasionally until vegetables are tender and top is lightly browned.

70. Baked Carrots And Potatoes With Nutmeg Recipe

Serving: 2 | Prep: | Cook: 60mins | Ready in:

Ingredients

- 1/2 c onions, chopped
- 2 tb vegetable broth
- 4 md carrots, peeled, julienned
- 4 md potatoes, peeled, julienned
- salt And pepper, to taste
- nutmeg, grated, for garnish
- 1 c milk, Skim

Direction

- In pan, sauté onions in the vegetable broth. Place half of carrots in a casserole dish that has been sprayed with non-stick cooking spray. Top with half of the potatoes and all of the onions. Sprinkle with salt, pepper and nutmeg. Repeat with remaining vegetables. Pour in the skim milk. Cover and bake at 350 deg. F for 50-60 min. or until vegetables are done and liquid is absorbed.

71. Baked Chicken Breasts And Potatoes Recipe

Serving: 2 | Prep: | Cook: 45mins | Ready in:

Ingredients

- chicken breasts (1 or 2 pieces per person depending on their size)
- 4-6 bigger potatoes, preferably a sweeter type
- milk
- creamy, spreadable cheese, not very salty (one of those you can spread on bread easily)
- pepper and paprika spice (sweet, not chilli) or a mix of spices for grilling

Direction

- Set the oven to 250°C and let it heat up while you work. Wash the chicken breasts, if they are too big, slice them in halves. Gather your spices and rub them onto the chicken breasts. Peel the potatoes and wash them thoroughly. Chop the potatoes into 4-6 parts (depends on their size). Try to have them chopped into somewhat even pieces, that'll make the baking easier to keep an eye on.
- Put a layer of aluminium foil on a cooking pan or a cookie sheet with raised edges. I suggest using two, one for the chicken and one for the potatoes, because the chicken will leak juices and that could ruin the potatoes. You should bend the edges of the aluminium foil upwards so no juices from the chicken will run off the foil on the pan/sheet.
- Note: For this recipe, it is crucial that you can blow hot air on the chicken and potatoes intensively. A convection type oven has a fan for this. It's very useful if you don't want to add any oil yet you want to make the potatoes slightly crispy. If you don't have it, it might not matter much, but you may need to bake the potatoes a bit longer to have them somewhat crispy.
- If the oven is heated up to 250°C, put in the potatoes (into the middle) and the chicken pan/sheet above the potatoes. Turn on the fan

for about 8-10 minutes. After that, turn off the fan and set the oven to 200°C, it should be near this temperature by now anyway.
- Get the potato sheet out, turn the potatoes over and put that sheet back into the oven.
- Let it bake for about 10-15 minutes, after this, check whether the potatoes or the chicken need to be turned around. It's a good idea to do that for the potatoes, it's usually not necessary for the chicken, but you've better off safe than sorry. After this, put them in for another 10-15 minutes.
- Now we can start making a cheese 'sauce'. It's basically milk, molten cheese (non-spreadable cheese often doesn't completely melt, which is what I like to avoid here). Get a small pot and put a bit of milk in it. There should be a layer of milk, about 1 cm thick. Start heating the milk up. When it starts boiling or it's close to boiling, add some cheese. Not all of it, as you'll probably want to go slow on this and if it's the first time you're making this, you'll need to decide how thick the cheese sauce should be. I like it when it's a thick liquid, so I add a bit more milk sometimes. If you have spreadable cheese triangles, start with 4 of them and the amount of milk I mentioned before. When the cheese melts, you can decide how much more and how thick you want it to be.
- The sauce, chicken and potatoes should be all done in about the same time. You can serve them immediately.
- Note: you probably don't want to add any spices on the potatoes. Salt is not necessary in this recipe, as there's lots of it in the cheese. This way, you can enjoy the true taste of baked sweetish potatoes and have a nice piece of meat to it. If you go with a different sauce, you can have a pretty low fat meal. You can use a marinade for the chicken if you don't want a sauce or anything else to go with it.

72. Baked Dill Potatoes Recipe

Serving: 6 | Prep: | Cook: 30mins | Ready in:

Ingredients

- 6 large baking potaoes
- Ground dill
- 1/4 - 1/2 cup melted butter
- seasoning salt
- garlic powder
- caynne pepper (or paprika)

Direction

- Wash potatoes and poke all over with fork
- Place on microwave safe dish (3-4 at a time)
- Cook on high for 10 min
- While the next set is being cooked
- Slice potatoes in 1/4 slice but not all the way through
- Place on square of foil
- Drizzle melted butter over potato
- Then sprinkle with dill, salt, garlic, and pepper
- Wrap. Repeat until they are all wrapped than place on warming rack on bbq while your meat is cooking!!
- Serve with sour cream
- Enjoy

73. Baked Eggs In Potato Recipe

Serving: 3 | Prep: | Cook: 25mins | Ready in:

Ingredients

- 1 medium potato
- 1 T butter
- 1/2 cup shredded cheese - more or less to taste
- 3 eggs
- salt and pepper
- heavy cream

Direction

- Wash and peel the potato and cut it into chunks. Place the potato in a pot of water, bring to a boil and cook until fork-tender, about 12 minutes.
- Drain the potato, then put in a medium-sized bowl. Mash the potato, adding butter and a little bit of cream (about 1 T) until you get the right consistency. Season with salt and pepper and add a little bit of cheese (about a 1/4 cup).
- Mix well.
- Spray 3 10-oz. ramekins (standard size) with cooking spray and dive the potato mixture between them, pushing down with the back of the spoon so that you create a well in the bottom.
- Next you can simply crack one egg into each well and top with cheese or you may beat each egg with a bit of cream and add the cheese to the beaten mixture, then pour it into the ramekins. My kids prefer the texture of the egg when it's beaten, although I like the traditional baked eggs.
- Place the ramekins in a pan or on a cookie sheet and bake in a preheated 400 degree oven for about 25 minutes or until the eggs are set.
- BEWARE: If you beat the eggs, cream and cheese instead of just plopping in a while egg, the mixture will puff up when it cooks. This is why setting the ramekins in a pan or on a sheet helps.

74. Baked Eggs In Potatoes Recipe

Serving: 4 | Prep: | Cook: 90mins | Ready in:

Ingredients

- 4 lg baking potatoes
- 1/4 c butter
- salt & pepper
- 1/2 c Grated cheese
- 4 sm eggs
- 1/4 c heavy cream
- 2 ts Chopped chives

Direction

- Preheat oven to 350 degrees. Scrub and dry potatoes, place on a baking sheet and rub a little oil or butter over skins. Place on baking sheets, bake 1 to 1 1/4 hours. Remove from oven.
- Cut a slice lengthwise off each potato. Scoop out insides. Mash scooped out potatoes in a bowl with remaining butter and seasoning beat cheese into potato mixture. Press mixture back into shells, leaving a hollow in centre large enough for an egg. Season and spoon the cream over. Return to the oven. Bake 8 to 10 minutes until eggs are lightly set. Sprinkle the chives and serve.

75. Baked German Potato Salad Recipe

Serving: 8 | Prep: | Cook: 30mins | Ready in:

Ingredients

- Baked German potato Salad
- 1 cup sliced bacon
- 1 cup chopped onion
- 3 tablespoons flour
- 2/3 cup vinegar
- 1 1/3 cup water
- 1 cup diced celery
- 3 teaspoons salt
- 2/3 cup sugar
- 1/2 teaspoon pepper
- 8 cups sliced cooked potatoes

Direction

- Fry the bacon. Drain and return 4 tablespoons fat to skillet. Add the celery, onion, salt, and flour. Cook gently. Add sugar, vinegar, pepper, and water; bring to a boil. Pour over potatoes and bacon into a 3-quart casserole. Cover and bake at 350 degrees for 30 minutes.

76. Baked New Potato Salad With Peanuts And Mustard Dressing Recipe

Serving: 8 | Prep: | Cook: 45mins | Ready in:

Ingredients

- 1/3 cup red skinned peanuts
- 2 pounds small red new potatoes scrubbed
- 1 tablespoon olive oil
- 1/8 teaspoon salt
- 1 teaspoon freshly ground black pepper
- 1 tablespoon rice wine vinegar
- 1/3 cup minced red onion
- 1 large carrot sliced on the diagonal
- 2 medium ribs celery sliced on the diagonal
- 1/2 cup mayonnaise
- 1/2 cup plain yogurt
- 2 tablespoons finely chopped fresh cilantro
- 1 tablespoon grainy mustard
- 1 tablespoon Dijon mustard
- 1/2 teaspoon ground cumin

Direction

- Put peanuts in a small baking pan and toast in a preheated 350 degree oven for 5 minutes.
- Cool slightly then rub in a kitchen towel to remove skins and chop coarsely.
- Cut potatoes into quarters and place in a baking pan then toss with olive oil, salt and pepper.
- Bake at 375 for 30 minutes stirring occasionally.
- Remove from oven and toss with vinegar then cool.
- Place red onion in a small bowl and cover with ice water.
- Let sit 20 minutes to reduce acidity.
- Drain and squeeze out the excess moisture with a paper towel.
- Bring a small pan of water to a boil then add carrots and cook 2 minutes.
- Drain and rinse with cold water to stop cooking then pat dry.
- Combine cooled potatoes, onion, carrots and celery in a large bowl.
- Stir together mayonnaise, yogurt, cilantro, mustards, cumin and several grindings black pepper.
- Combine with vegetables and refrigerate then stir in peanuts just before serving.

77. Baked New Red Potatoes Recipe

Serving: 4 | Prep: | Cook: 40mins | Ready in:

Ingredients

- 3 pounds new red potatoes -washed
- 1 stick butter
- 1/4 cup olive oil
- season salt

Direction

- Cut potatoes in half or quarter if they are larger
- Put in a large zip lock baggie
- Pour melted butter in bag
- Pour olive oil in bag
- Close the bag.
- Shake potatoes in butter and oil until covered.
- Spread on a greased baking sheet with sides.
- Sprinkle season salt over potatoes
- Bake 425 degrees for approx. 40 min.

78. Baked Old Bay Potato Sticks Recipe

Serving: 4 | Prep: | Cook: 30mins | Ready in:

Ingredients

- 2 to 3 large baking potatoes, scrubbed (peel if desired)
- 1/4 cup canola oil
- 1/4 cup fine dry breadcrumbs
- 2 tsp Old Bay Seasoning
- sour cream and ketchup to serve with potatoes

Direction

- Preheat oven to 400° F.
- Combine breadcrumbs and Old Bay Seasoning in large plastic bag.
- Cut potatoes lengthwise into 8 wedges.
- Roll pieces in canola oil.
- Add a few potatoes to the bag and shake to coat.
- Place potatoes skin side down on a baking sheet.
- Bake until potatoes are tender, about 30 minutes (depends on thickness of potato wedges - if cut thin, reduce baking time).

79. Baked Potato Bar Recipe

Serving: 4 | Prep: | Cook: 25mins | Ready in:

Ingredients

- Potatoes:
- 4 medium russet potatoes with a couple of fork punctures in each
- 1 teaspoon canola oil
- 6 slices turkey bacon
- Toppings:
- 1 cup shredded, reduced-fat sharp cheddar cheese
- 1/2 cup fat-free sour cream
- 4 green onions (the white and part of the green), chopped; or 1/4 cup chopped chives
- black pepper to taste
- 2 cups broccoli florets, steamed (optional)
- 4 strips crisp turkey bacon, broken into bits (optional)
- mushroom slices, sautéed in wine or broth (optional)

Direction

- Preheat oven to 400 degrees. Place potatoes into microwave/convection oven and set it to sensor cook for "hard vegetables" (or microwave on HIGH for about 10 minutes or until tender). Rub a little oil on the outside of each potato. Set them on a baking sheet and let the outside crisp up in the hot oven for 15 minutes.
- Set out all of your potato fixings on the table along with the baked potatoes (options include shredded cheese, sour cream, green onions, black pepper, broccoli florets, crisp turkey bacon broken into bits, sautéed mushrooms, etc.)

80. Baked Potato Discs Recipe

Serving: 1 | Prep: | Cook: 90mins | Ready in:

Ingredients

- 1 large brown potato per person
- Vegetable oil
- Creole seasoning
- Onion powder

Direction

- Wash potato skin good.
- Slice the potato into ½ inch discs, discarding both ends.
- Rinse the discs with cool water and dry with a paper towel.
- Place the discs into a bowl and completely cover with vegetable oil.
- Let potato soak in oil for 30 minutes.
- Preheat oven to 325 deg.
- Remove potato from oil and place on cookie sheet.
- Lightly sprinkle Creole seasoning and onion powder on potato discs.
- Cook potato discs for 20 minutes.

- Remove potato discs from oven, flip each potato discs and lightly sprinkle Creole seasoning and onion powder on potato discs again.
- Cook for about another 10minutes or until the potato discs are done.
- Remove from oven and enjoy.

81. Baked Potato Eggs Recipe

Serving: 4 | Prep: | Cook: 75mins | Ready in:

Ingredients

- 2 large baking potatoes
- 2 Tbs butter
- 1/4 cup grated parmesan cheese
- 2 precooked turkey sausages, diced
- 4 large eggs
- (I salted and peppered as well)

Direction

- Heat oven to 400F.
- Scrub the potatoes and pierce each with the tines of a fork. Bake until fork-tender, about 45 minutes.
- Carefully cut each potato in half. Scoop out the insides and stir in the butter and cheese. Fold in the sausages. Spoon the mixture back into the potato halves, creating a hollow in each centre. Break one egg into each hollow.
- Arrange on a baking sheet (I put aluminum foil on the sheet and sprayed the foil with cooking spray). Cook 10 to 15 minutes until set.
- **I'm not certain an egg will set in 10 minutes at 400F. Another reason why I raised my oven temperature. There was a tip with this recipe: Save time by poaching the eggs while the potatoes bake. Then slide the poached eggs on top instead of baking the eggs with the potatoes. (This sounds like a good tip to me!)

82. Baked Potato Hint Recipe

Serving: 4 | Prep: | Cook: 35mins | Ready in:

Ingredients

- baking potatoes
- 3 cups salt
- water

Direction

- When preparing baked potatoes for a dinner, try this:
- In a large pot place 3 cups of salt, the potatoes for the meal and enough water to cover by 2" over the potatoes (use more pots if they don't all fit), Boil the potatoes until cooked through, then bake as usual. The heavy salt content of the boiling solution causes the water to boil at a higher temperature than the normal 212 degrees, and produces a more fluffy texture to the potato after it is baked. It also adds a slight salt crust to the outside peel after baking.

83. Baked Potato Pizza Recipe

Serving: 6 | Prep: | Cook: 25mins | Ready in:

Ingredients

- 3 medium potatoes, peeled and cut into 1/8-inch slices
- 1 loaf (1 pound) frozen pizza dough, thawed
- 3 tablespoons reduced-fat butter
- 4 garlic cloves, minced
- 1/4 teaspoon salt
- 1/4 teaspoon pepper
- 1 cup (4 ounces) shredded part-skim mozzarella cheese
- 1/4 cup shredded parmigiano-reggiano cheese
- 6 turkey bacon strips, cooked and crumbled
- 2 green onions, chopped
- 2 tablespoons minced chives

- reduced-fat sour cream, optional

Direction

- Place potatoes in a small saucepan and cover with water. Bring to a boil. Reduce heat; cover and simmer for 15 minutes or until tender. Drain and pat dry.
- Unroll dough onto a 14-in. pizza pan coated with cooking spray; flatten dough and build up edges slightly. In a microwave-safe bowl, melt butter with garlic; brush over dough.
- Arrange potato slices in a single layer over dough; sprinkle with salt and pepper. Top with cheeses. Bake at 400° for 22-28 minutes or until crust is golden and cheese is melted.
- Sprinkle with bacon, onions and chives. Serve with sour cream if desired.
- Yield: 12 pieces.

84. Baked Potato Recipe

Serving: 1 | Prep: | Cook: 90mins | Ready in:

Ingredients

- potato

Direction

- Wrap in aluminium foil
- Bake. 180*c, 90 minutes or BBQ

85. Baked Potato Salad Recipe

Serving: 8 | Prep: | Cook: 20mins | Ready in:

Ingredients

- 5 lbs russet or red potatoes, peeled and cubed
- 3 stalks celery, chopped
- 1 red onion, chopped
- 6 slices bacon, cooked crisp and crumbled
- 8 oz. shredded cheddar cheese
- 8 oz. sour cream
- 1 cup sliced green onions
- 1 cup mayonnaise
- 1 tablespoon cracked black pepper
- salt to taste
- creole spice, just a dash will do!

Direction

- Boil potatoes until tender.
- Place potatoes, celery, onion, and green onions in large bowl.
- Stir in sour cream, mayonnaise, and cheese.
- Season with salt and pepper.
- Sprinkle with crumbled bacon and sprinkle with a little creole spice.

86. Baked Potato Skins Like TGIFridays And Ruby Tuesdays Recipe

Serving: 5 | Prep: | Cook: 25mins | Ready in:

Ingredients

- 10 Baked Potato Skins Halves (empty of potato) or quartered if the potatoes are really big
- 1 Tbsp.. Melted butter
- seasoned Salt
- 1 green onion Diced (can ommit)
- 1/2 C. Fried bacon Diced and Crispy Fried (about 5 strips)
- 3/4 C. Shredder cheddar cheese (I use jack & cheddar mix like Ruby Tuesday does)
- sour cream
- ranch dressing

Direction

- Heat oven to 375
- Brush potato shells with melted butter and sprinkle season all to taste

- Bake for 15 - 20 minutes until crisp but not dry and hard.
- Remove and sprinkle with cheese, bacon and onion
- Place back in oven until cheese is melted.
- Serve with sour cream and Ranch dressing.
- Since I have a deep fryer, the way I do it is too deep fry the potato skins after they are already baked and the potato meat is scooped out (like Ruby Tuesday does). Just for a couple minutes to make them crispy, then I continue with the recipe omitting the baking for 15-20 min. But just putting them in the oven to melt the cheese.
- Really oven or frying is both fine, we just have a habit of doing it like we did at Ruby's since we've been making these long before I found this recipe.

87. Baked Potato Skins Recipe

Serving: 8 | Prep: | Cook: 33mins | Ready in:

Ingredients

- 4 large baked baking potatoes
- 3 tbsp. of vegetable oil
- 1 tbsp. of grated parmesan cheese
- 1/2 tsp of salt
- 1/4 tsp of garlic powder
- 1/4 tsp of paprika
- 1/8 tsp of pepper
- 8 slices of cooked and crumbled bacon
- 2 c. of shredded cheddar cheese
- 1/2 c. of sour cream, optional
- 4 sliced green onions

Direction

- First you need to cut the potatoes in half lengthwise; scoop out pulp and put the rest in the trash.
- Make sure to leave 1/4-inch shell.
- Next put these on a greased baking sheet.

- Now add the parmesan cheese, salt, garlic powder, paprika and pepper and brush this over potato skins.
- Now bake at 475* for approx. 8 minutes and turn over.
- Bake for another 8 minutes or so and then turn right side up.
- Then you can sprinkle bacon and cheddar on the skins.
- Then you can cook approx. 2 minutes longer or until cheese is melted.
- Add cheese on top and serve!

88. Baked Potato Slims Recipe

Serving: 4 | Prep: | Cook: 35mins | Ready in:

Ingredients

- 1/4 c. water
- 2 tbsp. vegetable oil
- 1/2 tsp. Tabasco pepper sauce
- 4 med. potatoes OR 1 pkg. (9 oz.) frozen french fries
- 1/4 c. grated Romano Or parmesan cheese
- 1 env. Shake 'n Bake seasoned coating mix for chicken
- aluminum foil

Direction

- Mix water with oil and Tabasco.
- Peel potatoes and cut into 1/2 inch strips or use frozen French fries. Toss potatoes in water, oil and Tabasco mixture.
- Mix cheese with shake 'n bake in bag.
- Place 8 to 10 strips in bag at one time.
- Shake until evenly coated.
- Place potatoes in a single layer on a cookie sheet lined with foil. Bake in preheated oven at 400 degrees for 30 to 35 minutes (20 to 25 for frozen).

89. Baked Potato Taco Recipe

Serving: 4 | Prep: | Cook: 5mins | Ready in:

Ingredients

- As needed:
- .
- potatoes
- hamburger, browned and drained
- lettuce, shredded
- tomatoes, chopped
- onions, chopped
- cheese, grated
- black olives, sliced
- sour cream
- Jalapena peppers
- Anything else you desire

Direction

- This is the same as a regular taco, just substitute the tortilla with a baked potato.
- Bake as many potatoes as needed in the microwave (time varies with ovens)
- While hot, slice open the top and stuff in whatever fillings you want.
- Pop it in the micro for a few more seconds until the cheese is melted.
- All done.

90. Baked Potato Wedges Recipe

Serving: 4 | Prep: | Cook: 50mins | Ready in:

Ingredients

- 3 large russet potatoes-unpeeled
- 1/4 cup olive or canola oil
- 2 tablespoons parmesean cheese
- 1/2 - 1 teaspoon salt
- 1 teaspoon pepper
- 1 teaspoon garlic powder
- 1/2 teaspoon paprika
- 1/2 teapoon cayenne pepper

Direction

- Preheat oven to 400 degrees.
- Cut potatoes lengthwise into wedges. Set aside.
- In a large mixing bowl, combine remaining ingredients. Mix well.
- Add potato wedges and toss to coat.
- Place in a single layer on a large baking sheet lined with foil.
- Bake for 25 minutes, turn wedges over, and bake for an additional 25 minutes or until crisp outside and tender inside.
- Serve immediately.

91. Baked Potato With Vegetable Soup Recipe

Serving: 0 | Prep: | Cook: 1hours | Ready in:

Ingredients

- basic ingredient:
- 5 pieces rosit potato
- 2 medium white onion
- 11/2 cups vegetable stock
- 1/2 cup milk
- 1 tbsp olive oil
- oregano flakes
- salt and black pepper
- 1 cup of parmessan cheese

Direction

- Heat oven in 180 degrees.
- 1. Cut potato thinly used potato slicer in round shape or according to the potato shapes, soak it in the water to avoid discoloration.
- 2. Cut onions in round shape, thinly
- 3. Boil the stock, and simmer for 5 minutes; then add the milk and continue stirring in 5 minutes or until stock will thicken.
- 4. Heat little oil, enough to wet the pan and sauté onion (it is best to caramelized it)
- 5. Rub the pan 4x9" with an olive oil

- 6. lay the potato nicely, sprinkle salt and pepper on top, onion, cheese, and pour the stock on top...it should be repeated 3 times.
- 7. Any left for stock; pour it on top of the last layer; covered with cheese and sprinkle with oregano flakes. Drizzle with olive oil.
- 8. Bake it for 25 minutes or until the stock is gone and potato are cook.
- It's best to avoid it turning into brown, and too dry. Little creamy is best.

92. Baked Potato And Cheese Balls Recipe

Serving: 4 | Prep: | Cook: 20mins | Ready in:

Ingredients

- 6 tablespoons butter, divided
- 3 cups shredded potatoes or 1 bag shredded hash brown potatoes, thawed
- 1 medium onion, chopped
- 1 tablespoon garlic, minced
- 1/2 cup mozzarella cheese, shredded
- 1/2 cup monterey jack cheese, shredded
- 1/4 teaspoon italian seasoning
- salt and pepper to taste

Direction

- In a large skillet, melt 3 tablespoons butter.
- Add potatoes.
- Cook until brown.
- Remove and put into a large bowl.
- To the same skillet, add remaining butter, onions and garlic.
- Cook until golden brown, be careful not to burn.
- Add this mixture to the potato mixture.
- Add cheeses.
- Mix well.
- With an ice cream scooper, pack well and scoop potato mixture onto a greased cookie sheet.
- Broil until golden brown and hot.

93. Baked Potato Bacon And Chives Bread Recipe

Serving: 0 | Prep: | Cook: 40mins | Ready in:

Ingredients

- 1/2 cup mashed potatoes
- 3 to 4 cups all-purpose unbleached flour (I'll explain the ambiguity below)
- 3/4 cup water
- 1/2 cup sour cream
- 2 teaspoons instant yeast
- 1 teaspoon salt
- 1/4 cup cooked bacon
- 1/2 cup chopped fresh chives

Direction

- To begin, chop up two or three slices of bacon and fry them up. Remove them from the heat.
- Mix the mashed potatoes, yeast, salt, and 2 cups of the flour together in a large mixing bowl or the bowl of an electric mixer. . Add the sour cream, water, chives, and bacon and mix together until all ingredients are combined. I also mixed in the bacon fat, which there was about a tablespoon of in the pan, because it improves the flavour of the loaf.
- At this point you'll have a very wet, sticky mess, probably more of a batter than a dough. Add additional flour a handful (1/8 cup) at a time and mix or knead it in.
- (I lost track of exactly how much extra flour I added, but it seems like it was around 9 or 10 hands full. I added 4 or 5 hands full and mixed them in while the dough was still in the bowl, then I poured the dough out onto a well-floured cutting board and added more, kneading it with my hands which I repeatedly dipped in flour to keep the dough from sticking to them. After 5 or 10 minutes of this I ended up with something that was still quite sticky, but was definitely in the realm of a

dough and not a batter: it could be formed into a ball and generally held its shape.)
- Once you have combined the ingredients well and gotten the balance of flour and water to a level that seems acceptable, return the dough to a well-oiled bowl. Cover the bowl with plastic wrap and allow the dough to rise for 90 minutes at room temperature or until it has doubled in size.
- Remove the dough from the bowl and shape the loaf or loaves. Notice how moist and gummy my dough was when I cut it to shape it into two loaves:
- One probably could add more flour and make an acceptable loaf of bread with a drier dough, but I've been finding that I get better results the wetter I am able to leave it. But this really is an art, not a science, so use your own best judgement.
- At this point you need to shape the loaves, cover them loosely and let them rise until they double in size again, about 45 minutes. You could put them in greased baking pans and let them rise and bake them in those. I wanted round loaves, so I put them in a couple of couche lined baskets:
- Professional bakers use these kinds of baskets I got from a neighbour who works in bakery. It works very well, but you can fake the same thing with a well-floured kitchen towel (the linen kind, not a fuzzy one).
- I placed the baskets on a table, the couche over the baskets, and the dough in the floured couche in the baskets. I wrapped the edges of the couche around the balls of dough and let them rise. When they had risen I simply unwrapped the loaves and shook them out of the couche onto my peel (which I dust with semolina flour) and threw them into the oven.
- While the loaves are rising again, preheat the oven to 425. If you have a baking stone, be sure to put it in early to heat.
- When they have doubled in size (as I said before, about 45 minutes after shaping), put the loaves in the oven to bake. I baked them at 425 for 5 minutes and then reduce the temperature to 350 and baked them another half an hour. The loaves are done when the internal temperature reaches the 185 to 195 degree range (as read with an instant-read thermometer) or when they are nice and brown on the outside and sound hollow when tapped on the bottom. For me this took about 35 minutes.

94. Baked Potatoe Strips Recipe

Serving: 0 | Prep: | Cook: 45mins | Ready in:

Ingredients

- large potatoes(or as many as you want)
- melted butter or margerine
- cornflake crumbs

Direction

- Peel large potatoes (you can make as many as you want)
- Cut into strips as for French fries
- Dip each strip in melted butter
- Roll in fine cornflake crumbs
- Place in a single layer on a greased cookie sheet or a shallow baking dish
- Sprinkle with sea salt or regular salt
- Bake in a 375 degree oven for about 45 min., or until done

95. Baked Potatoes Simply Become Salad Recipe

Serving: 1 | Prep: | Cook: 40mins | Ready in:

Ingredients

- potato of choice
- olive oil
- butter
- lemon to squeeze
- sea salt

- fresh ground black pepper
- and ground sumac tastes great and looks good too
- fresh herbs
- sour cream or feta cheese
- optional slices of cherry tomatoes or sundried tomatoes or olives or...

Direction

- Bake your potato
- (Or a whole bag - full)
- Refrigerate over night
- Cut in half
- Now, you will see the potato has a heart (aw!)
- Stick your thumb in the heart and the potato will easily split into quarters.
- Drizzle with olive oil
- Salt and pepper to taste
- Chunks of butter if you love it
- Squeeze lemon juice over top
- Top with sour cream or feta cheese and sprinkling of fresh cut herbs.
- Garnish with optionals
- Sumac is my favorite part - sprinkled over the potato and then over the sour cream and toppings too.

96. Baked Potatoes Stuffed With Spinach Parmesan And Mushrooms Recipe

Serving: 6 | Prep: | Cook: 50mins | Ready in:

Ingredients

- 6 large baked potatoes
- 1 package frozen spinach thawed
- 1-1/4 cup grated parmesan cheese
- 1-3/4 cup sliced mushrooms
- 6 tablespoons butter
- 1/2 teaspoon salt
- 1 teaspoon freshly ground black pepper

Direction

- Bake potatoes then cut in half and scoop out pulp with a spoon.
- Place pulp in a bowl with two thirds of the butter.
- Place potato shells in a baking dish.
- Sauté mushrooms in the remaining third butter and add salt.
- Thaw spinach or heat on low until just thawed then drain completely.
- Mash and blend potato and butter together until well blended.
- Add cheese, spinach and mushrooms then spoon mixture back into potato shells.
- Bake at 350 for 15 minutes then serve immediately.

97. Baked Potatoes Stuffed With Bacon Anchovies And Sage Recipe

Serving: 4 | Prep: | Cook: 60mins | Ready in:

Ingredients

- 4 medium-sized waxy potatoes, skin left on
- olive oil sea salt 4 slices bacon
- 8 fresh sage leaves
- 4 good quality anchovy fillets in oil, drained
- 1 clove garlic--slice in fourths, lengthwise
- 1 lemon

Direction

- Preheat oven to 400 degrees.
- Using either a pineapple or apple corer, or a conventional peeler, stick the tool into a potato and twist it round and round as you cut through, as if you are coring an apple--you're trying to carve out a tube from inside the potato. Keep cores because they will plug the stuffing inside the potato. Prick with fork or knife a few times, and give them an oil and sea salt rub.

- Lay out the stuffing for each potato: a slice of bacon topped with 2 sage leaves, an anchovy fillet, and a sliver of garlic. Grate over some lemon zest. Fold and twist the stuffing together into a little sausage shape and stuff into each potato. Don't worry if you have bits sticking out at either end.
- Cut the saved plugs in half and stuff them back in either end of each potato to keep the stuffing in place. Place on a baking tray for about an hour, turning every so often, until crisp, golden and cooked.
- Serves 4.
- per serving: 289 kcal; 17 gm. fat; 28 g carbohydrates; 313 mg sodium; 17 mg cholesterol.

98. Baked Potatoes Stuffed With Crabmeat Recipe

Serving: 6 | Prep: | Cook: 90mins | Ready in:

Ingredients

- 6 baking potatoes
- 6 ounces crab meat
- 1/2 cup half & half
- 2 tablespoons butter, melted
- salt, to taste
- cayenne pepper, to taste
- 1 onion, grated
- 8 ounces cheddar cheese, freshly grated

Direction

- Preheat oven to 375°. Pierce each potato several times with a fork and bake for 45 to 60 minutes. Remove potatoes from oven and cool slightly. Cut each in half and scoop out insides, leaving skins intact. Place potato filling in a medium mixing bowl; set potato shells aside.
- Reduce oven to 350°. To the potato filling, add crabmeat, half & half, butter, salt, cayenne pepper and onion and whip until smooth.

Return potato mixture to potato shells and top with cheese. Bake for 30 minutes or until cheese is bubbly

99. Baked Potatoes With Olives And Feta Recipe

Serving: 4 | Prep: | Cook: 35mins | Ready in:

Ingredients

- 4 small russet potatoes
- 1/3 c Greek yogurt
- 1/2 c feta cheese
- 4 tsp. chopped pitted kalamata olives

Direction

- Preheat oven to 450'
- With a fork prick potatoes (2lbs total) in several places.
- Place potatoes on a plate and microwave till tender when pierced with a knife, 7 to 10 mins.
- Transfer to rimmed baking sheet and bake till skin is crisp, about 10 mins.
- Halve potatoes. Dividing evenly, top halves with yogurt, feta and olives. Season with coarse salt and ground pepper. Sprinkle with fresh chopped chives.

100. Baked Potatoes On The Grill Recipe

Serving: 4 | Prep: | Cook: 70mins | Ready in:

Ingredients

- 4 Med - Lg potatoes, your choice (We like red ones)
- EVOO
- kosher salt
- aluminum foil

- GARNISHES
- butter
- cheese
- Sourcream
- chives
- bacon bits, or, bacon fried and crumbled
- salt
- fresh ground black pepper

Direction

- Preheat grill to medium heat
- Scrub potatoes well, so you can eat the crispy skins!
- Poke several holes in each potato with a fork
- Lay out a piece of foil on the counter for each potato (to minimize the messiness that will ensue), shiny side up
- Lay a potatoes on each piece of foil
- Drizzle each with about 2 T EVOO
- Generously sprinkle each with kosher salt
- Pick up potatoes and rub oil and salt all over
- Wrap tightly in foil, shiny side to potato
- Place on top rack of grill, or, turn heat off of one side, and place on the side with no heat
- Grill about 35 minutes with lid closed
- Turn halfway over
- Grill another 35 minutes or so
- Check for doneness with fork
- Should slide in with no resistance
- Garnish as desired and enjoy!!

101. Baked Potatoes With Cornmeal Recipe

Serving: 4 | Prep: | Cook: 15mins | Ready in:

Ingredients

- 4 medium sized potatoes washed thoroughly
- salt
- 1/2 cup cornmeal
- 1/4 cup chopped garlic
- 4 Tbsp olive oil
- 2 Tbsp shallots/spring onion

Direction

- Cute potatoes into slices 2-3cm thick. Season with salt and roll generously in cornmeal and garlic. Place onto a greased baking tray and sprinkle with oil. Bake in preheated 180 d C oven until cooked, light golden in colour and crispy. Sprinkle with shallots.

102. Baked Potatoes With Dreams Of Glory Recipe

Serving: 1 | Prep: | Cook: 40mins | Ready in:

Ingredients

- 1 large baked potato
- 1/2 cup sauteed diced mushrooms
- 1 egg yolk
- 1/4 cup sour cream
- 1/4 cup grated parmesan cheese

Direction

- Wrap a tea towel and press gently to soften 1 large baked potato.
- Cut a small hole in the side and scoop out the inside.
- Mix the potato with 1/2 cup sautéed diced mushrooms, 1 egg yolk, 1/4 cup sour cream, 1/4 cup grated Parmesan cheese until it is very fluffy and lump less.
- Scoop it back into the potato shell, reheat in a hot oven for about 10 minutes, and serve with a little paprika on top.

103. Baked Rosti Potatoes Recipe

Serving: 8 | Prep: | Cook: 90mins | Ready in:

Ingredients

- 2 TB oil
- 2 pkg. (20 oz. ea.) refrigerated shredded hash browns
- 1-1/2 c shredded cheddar cheese
- 1/2 c flour
- 1 small onion, grated
- 1/2 tsp black pepper
- 1 egg, beaten

Direction

- Preheat oven to 400'
- Brush oil onto bottom and up sides of 13x9" baking dish. Combine all remaining ingredients except egg. Add egg; mix lightly. Press onto bottom of baking dish.
- Bake 55 mins to 1 hour or till golden brown. Let stand 10 mins before cutting to serve.
- Make ahead: Bake potato-egg mixture ahead of time. Cool, cover and refrigerate up to 24 hours.
- When ready to serve, bake uncovered, in a 350' oven for 15-20 mins. Or till heated thru.

104. Baked Spanish Potato Omelet Recipe

Serving: 1 | Prep: | Cook: 30mins | Ready in:

Ingredients

- 5 eggs
- 2 c. peeled, cooked, cubed potatoes
- 1 onion, finely chopped
- 1 green pepper, minced
- 12 green stuffed Spanish olives, slices
- 1 tsp. salt
- 4 oz. lean, cooked ham, cubed (see directions)

Direction

- Beat eggs until fluffy as can get, Fold in remaining ingredients. Spray a round, non-stick cake pan with cooking spray for no-fat frying. Spoon in omelet mixture. Bake at 350 degrees for 25 to 30 minutes until eggs are set. Cut into wedges. Instead of ham you can use roast, chicken or turkey even tuna or shrimp!

105. Baked Spicy Ham And Cheese Mashed Potatoes Recipe

Serving: 4 | Prep: | Cook: 15mins | Ready in:

Ingredients

- 2 cups mashed potatoes
- 3/4 teaspoon garlic salt
- 1 cup fully cooked ham, diced
- 1 cup shredded Cheddar cheese
- 1/2 cup heavy whipping cream, whipped
- 2 tablesppon jalapeno peppers diced

Direction

- Preheat oven to 450 degrees.
- In a large bowl, combine the mashed potatoes and garlic salt and peppers. Spread potatoes into a 1 1/2-quart casserole dish. Add in the ham.
- In a small bowl, fold the cheddar cheese into the heavy cream. Spoon mixture over ham layer.
- Bake for 15 minutes or until golden brown.

106. Baked Stuffed New Potatoes Recipe

Serving: 4 | Prep: | Cook: 45mins | Ready in:

Ingredients

- 700g new potatoes, scrubbed
- A little oil

- A little sea salt and freshly ground black pepper
- 6 tbsp creme fraiche
- 100g Seriously Strong cheddar cheese, grated
- 3 tbsp freshly chopped chives

Direction

- Preheat oven to 220 degrees, fan oven 200.
- Place the potatoes on a baking tray, drizzle over the olive oil and sprinkle the salt, then use your hands to rub it in all over the skins,
- Bake for about 40 mins or until tender.
- Whilst the potatoes cook, mix the crème fraiche, cheese and chives together with salt and pepper to taste. Chill until required.
- Remove potatoes from the oven, cut a cross in the top of each and fluff up the flesh.
- Place potatoes back on baking tray and spoon a little filling into each.
- Return to the oven for 5 minutes before serving,

107. Baked Sweet Potato Chips Recipe

Serving: 4 | Prep: | Cook: 35mins | Ready in:

Ingredients

- 2 pounds sweet potatoes peeled and sliced
- 1-1/2 teaspoon sugar
- 1-1/2 tablespoon lemon juice
- 1-1/2 teaspoon margarine melted
- 1 tablespoon freshly ground black pepper

Direction

- Combine all ingredients in a mixing bowl.
- Layer potatoes in a baking dish coated with non-stick cooking spray.
- Add any remaining liquid from bowl and cover dish with foil.
- Bake at 350 for 35 minutes.

108. Baked Sweet Potato Felafel Recipe

Serving: 6 | Prep: | Cook: 60mins | Ready in:

Ingredients

- 2 medium sweet potatoes (orange inside), around 700g or 1 1/2 pounds in total
- 1 1/2 teaspoons ground cumin
- 2 small cloves of garlic, chopped
- 1 1/2 teaspoons ground coriander
- 2 big handfuls of fresh cilantro/coriander, chopped
- juice of half a lemon
- a scant cup (120g) gram /chickpea flour
- a splash of olive oil
- a sprinkling of sesame seeds
- salt and pepper

Direction

- Preheat the oven to 425F degrees (220C) and roast the sweet potatoes whole until just tender - 45 minutes to 1 hour.
- Turn off the oven, leave the potatoes to cool, then peel.
- Put the sweet potatoes, cumin, garlic, ground and fresh coriander, lemon juice and gram/chickpea flour into a large bowl.
- Season well, and mash until smooth with no large chunks.
- Stick in the fridge to firm up for an hour, or the freezer for 20-30 minutes.
- When you take it out, your mix should be sticky rather than really wet.
- You can add a tablespoon or so more of chickpea flour if necessary (the water content of sweet potatoes varies enormously).
- Reheat the oven to 400F/200C.
- Using a couple of soup spoons (put a well-heaped spoonful of mix in one spoon and use the concave side of the other to shape the sides) or a falafel scoop if you have one, make

- the mixture into falafel looking things and put them on an oiled tray.
- Sprinkle sesame seeds on top and bake in the oven for around 15 minutes, until the bases are golden brown.
- Makes about 18 falafel, enough for 4 - 6.

109. Baked Sweet Potato Latkes Recipe

Serving: 12 | Prep: | Cook: 40mins | Ready in:

Ingredients

- Baked sweet potato Latkes (based on the recipe originally published in Women's Health Magazine)
- 2 pounds grated sweet potatoes
- 1 medium onion, grated
- 2 eggs, beaten
- 1/4 cup flour
- 1/4 tsp baking powder
- 1/2 tsp salt
- 1 tsp cinnamon
- 1/2 tsp nutmeg

Direction

- Preheat oven to 400°F. Spray a cookie sheet with non-stick spray or use a silpat.
- In a large bowl, combine all ingredients. Drop by 1/3-cupfuls onto cookie sheet. Flatten with spatula.
- Bake for 25 minutes; flip and bake for an additional 15 minutes.
- Serve with light sour cream and a dash of cinnamon and nutmeg.

110. Baked Sweet Potato Recipe

Serving: 2 | Prep: | Cook: 120mins | Ready in:

Ingredients

- 1 large sweet potato
- 1 stick fresh cinnamon
- 2 pats of butter
- Pinch of salt
- Pinch of nutmeg

Direction

- Wash the sweet potato well and bake in a toaster or conventional oven on 350 Degrees for 2 hours or until soft.
- Grind the cinnamon stick in your coffee grinder until powder like, same with the nutmeg.
- Slice the sweet potato into halves and salt to taste, add 1 pat of butter to each half and then sprinkle with the fresh ground cinnamon and nutmeg and serve.
- You won't believe how much flavour the cinnamon and nutmeg make this side dish fantastic!

111. Baked Sweet Potato With Cinnamon Chile Butter Recipe

Serving: 6 | Prep: | Cook: 60mins | Ready in:

Ingredients

- 1 stick unsalted butter softened
- 2 tablespoons New Mexico chili powder
- 1 tablespoon ground cinnamon
- 1/2 teaspoon salt
- 1/8 teaspoon cayenne pepper

Direction

- Using an electric mixer beat first 5 ingredients in medium bowl until fluffy.
- Preheat oven to 400F.
- Line large baking sheet with foil.
- Place sweet potatoes on sheet;
- Bake until tender about 1 hour or until done.

- Cut each sweet potato lengthwise and spoon 1 table spoon butter into each potato.
- Serve.

112. Baked Sweet Potato And Chile Wedges Recipe

Serving: 10 | Prep: | Cook: 25mins | Ready in:

Ingredients

- 3 1/2 pouns seet potatoes, about 5 or 6
- 2 tbsp olive oi
- 1 tsp sea salt
- 1/4 tsp pepper
- 1 tsp chili powder (use more if you like...I can't with my husband's tummy)
- 1 tbsp honey
- 1 (8 oz) container light sour cream
- 1/3 cup cilantro

Direction

- Preheat oven to 450 degrees. Cut each unpeeled potato into 1 inch thick wedges. Place in a plastic zip bag, toss with oil, salt and pepper.
- Arrange in two 13 x 9 inch pans.
- Meanwhile, in small bowl combine orange juice, chili powder, and honey; set aside
- Bake potatoes, uncovered, 25 to 30 minutes or until tender, brushing 3 times with the orange juice mixture, and shaking pan occasionally.
- Meanwhile, in a small bowl combine sour cream, 1/2 tsp. chili powder, and cilantro. Transfer potatoes to a serving dish; serve with sour cream mixture.

113. Baked Sweet Potatoes Recipe

Serving: 8 | Prep: | Cook: 50mins | Ready in:

Ingredients

- 6 sweet potatoes
- 1 (8 ounce) package cream cheese, softened
- 1/3 cup brown sugar, more or less to your liking.
- 1 tablespoon vanilla extract
- 1/3 cup chopped walnuts
- 1/2 cup butter
- 1/2 cup honey
- 1/2 cup orange juice
- Pinch salt and pepper

Direction

- In a small bowl, combine butter, honey, orange juice, nutmeg, salt and pepper; set aside. Peel sweet potatoes; cut into 1/2 inch thick slices. Cook sweet potatoes in saucepan of boiling, salted water until just tender; drain well. In greased 10 inch pie plate, or shallow casserole, arrange half of sweet potatoes. Pour half of the orange juice mixture over top. Arrange remaining sweet potato slices in alternating circles or rows on top. Drizzle with half of remaining orange juice mixture. Cover and refrigerate remaining O.J. mixture. Cover pie plate and refrigerate up to 24 hours. Let stand at room temperature 1 hour, then bake, covered, in 325F oven, for 45 to 50 minutes or until heated through. Heat reserved orange juice mixture until margarine has melted. Uncover pie plate, and brush vegetables with O.J. mixture; bake 5 minutes until lightly glazed In a large mixing bowl mash potatoes, meanwhile, in a large bowl combine cream cheese, brown sugar, margarine, vanilla, salt and pepper. Combine the two bowls, mix well and fold in walnuts. Spoon mixture into dish or dishes of your liking. Bake for 5 minutes, or until heated through. This also works well in ramekins topped with marshmallows and broiled.

114. Baked Sweet Potatoes With Bacon And Blue Cheese Recipe

Serving: 6 | Prep: | Cook: 20mins | Ready in:

Ingredients

- 4 medium sweet potatoes, peeled & diced
- 1/2 cup unsalted butter, melted
- 6 slices bacon, cooked and crumbled
- 1 cup blue cheese, crumbled
- salt & pepper to taste

Direction

- Preheat oven to 350.
- Over medium-high heat, boil the potatoes in enough water to cover until tender.
- Drain and return to the pot, add the butter and mash; season to taste.
- Turn the potatoes out into a large baking dish, top with blue cheese and the bacon.
- Place in the oven until the cheese is bubbly and the potatoes are heated through.

115. Baked Sweet Potatoes With Ginger And Honey Recipe

Serving: 12 | Prep: | Cook: 40mins | Ready in:

Ingredients

- 9 sweet potatoes, peeled and cubed
- 1/2 cup honey
- 3 tablespoons grated fresh ginger
- 2 tablespoons walnut oil
- 1 teaspoon ground cardamom
- 1/2 teaspoon ground black pepper

Direction

- Preheat oven to 400 degrees.
- In a large bowl, combine the sweet potatoes, honey, ginger, oil, cardamom and pepper.
- Transfer to a large cast iron frying pan.
- Bake for 20 minutes.
- Turn the mixture over to expose the pieces from the bottom of the pan.
- Bake for another 20 minutes, or until the sweet potatoes are tender and caramelized on the outside.

116. Baked Tex Mex Potato With Pico Degallo Recipe

Serving: 2 | Prep: | Cook: 20mins | Ready in:

Ingredients

- About 900 g roasted potatoes (I used small tricolor potatoes)(click here for the recipe, quartered the potato and omit the rosemary)
- 200 g Tex-Mex cheese (combination of jalapeno Jack, Cheddar, and mozzarella cheese)
- olive oil
- sea salt
- fresh ground black pepper
- 2 scallions, chopped
- pico de gallo-Mexican salsa
- for the salsa pico de gallo
- 4 Medium tomatoes, diced
- ½ (100 g) white onion, diced
- 2 serrano chilies, finely chopped
- 1 avocado, pitted and cubed
- A small bunch of cilantro, chopped
- ½ of a lime, juiced or to taste
- sea salt to taste

Direction

- Preheat the oven to 400°F.
- Lightly grease 4 small or 1 large shallow baking dishes with olive oil. Layer the potatoes in the baking dish followed by the cheese, sea salt, and black pepper. Repeat another layer.
- Bake the potatoes in the oven for about 8 to 10 minutes or until the cheese is nicely melted.

Remove from the oven, and top with chopped scallions. Serve the potatoes with Pico De Gallo.
- Method of Pico De Gallo:
- Combine the tomatoes, onion, chilies, avocado, cilantro, lime juice and season with sea salt. Let the salsa stand at a room temperature for about 10 minutes before serving.

117. Baked Tomatoes Stuffed With Cheesy Potatoes Recipe

Serving: 6 | Prep: | Cook: 15mins | Ready in:

Ingredients

- 6 large, firm, unpeeled tomatoes
- 3 cups mashed potatoes (using fresh potatoes or instant potato flakes prepared according to package directions)
- 1/4 cup fresh, chopped chives
- 1/2 teaspoon dried thyme
- 1 - 2 teaspoons pepper
- 1 1/4 cup shredded cheddar cheese, divided
- 1/4 cup dry bread crumbs
- 3 teaspoons paprika
- salt to taste

Direction

- Preheat oven to 350°F.
- Using a paring knife, remove the stem end of each tomato. Using a grapefruit spoon, small melon baller or a teaspoon, carefully hollow out each tomato, removing seeds and juice. Sprinkle the inside of each tomato with a little salt and place the tomatoes upside down on a cooling rack to drain for about 15 minutes.
- In a medium mixing bowl, combine the potatoes, chives, thyme, pepper and 1 cup of the cheddar cheese. Fill tomato cups with the potato mixture using a teaspoon.
- In a small bowl, combine bread crumbs, remaining 1/4 cup cheddar cheese and paprika; sprinkle on top of each tomato.
- Place filled tomatoes in non-stick or well-oiled muffin cups. Bake 10 - 15 minutes until topping is crisp and tomatoes are heated through.

118. Baked White Fish And Fingerling Potatoes Recipe

Serving: 2 | Prep: | Cook: 35mins | Ready in:

Ingredients

- potatoes
- 2 tablespoons olive oil, divided
- 1/2 pound fingerling potatoes, washed and cut into 1/2-inch slices
- 2 garlic cloves, minced
- 2 tablespoons fresh chives, minced
- sea salt, to taste
- ground pepper, to taste
- fish
- 3/4 cup dry white wine
- 1 tablespoon olive oil
- 1/4 cup lemon juice
- 1 tablespoon fresh tarragon or another of your favorite herbs, chopped
- 1 garlic clove, minced
- sea salt, to taste
- ground pepper, to taste
- 2 white fish fillets, 6 ounces each, skinned 2 thin lemon slices (for garnish)
- paprika for garnish

Direction

- Preheat oven to 400°F.
- In a large baking dish, cover the bottom with parchment paper and rub 1/4 teaspoon oil onto paper.
- Place potato slices in a single layer in baking dish and coat with remaining oil, garlic, chives, salt and pepper.
- Bake potatoes for 20 minutes. Remove dish from oven and flip potatoes over. Bake for another 15 minutes.

- While potatoes are cooking, mix together wine, olive oil, lemon juice, herbs, garlic, salt and pepper. Marinate fish in refrigerator for approximately 30 minutes.
- When potatoes are tender, remove dish from oven and push potatoes to the sides to make room for the fish to lie flat. Place fish in centre of dish and bake fish (with potatoes) until opaque but still moist, about 10 minutes. Garnish fish with lemon slices and sprinkle potatoes with paprika.

119. Baked Potato Salad Recipe

Serving: 10 | Prep: | Cook: 60mins | Ready in:

Ingredients

- 8-10 potatoes
- 1 cup mayonnaise (Miracle Whip does not do well)
- 1 lb velvetta
- 1/2 cup diced onion
- 1/2 cup cooked crumbled bacon or cheat like me and use bac o bits

Direction

- Boil potatoes whole in skin till slightly tender
- Peel skin (or leave on) and chunk potatoes
- In separate bowl mix all other ingredients together and pour over top of potatoes
- Bake at 350 for 1 hour

120. Baked Potatoes In The Crockpot Recipe

Serving: 12 | Prep: | Cook: 240mins | Ready in:

Ingredients

- 12 medium potatoes (washed and unpeeled)
- olive oil

Direction

- Fill a large crockpot with potatoes, drizzle a little olive oil over the top. Cover and cook on high for 4 hours.

121. Baked Potatoes With Apple Recipe

Serving: 4 | Prep: | Cook: 15mins | Ready in:

Ingredients

- 4 Large baking potatoes
- 1/2 Large Cooking apple. I usually use Bramleys
- 1 oz. margarine or butter
- 1 Large onion - finely chopped
- 4 sage leaves - chopped - or dried sage if fresh not available
- 1/2 Teaspoon of mustard powder
- salt to taste
- margarine for greasing pan

Direction

- Cook the Potatoes - You can either boil or cook in the Microwave
- Cut in half - lengthwise.
- Scoop the potato out and mash up well in a basin
- Peel, core and finely chop the apple
- Peel and finely chop the Onion
- Melt Margarine or Butter in a frying pan
- Fry the onion gently,
- Stir in the apple and cook for a further 2 - 3 minutes till soft.
- Mix the apple and onion mixture with the Potato mash
- Add the Sage, Mustard and Salt
- Spoon back into the Potato shells
- Put onto a greased shallow oven dish or tin

- Place in oven and Bake for 15 minutes.

122. Baked Potatoes With Cheese Cream Recipe

Serving: 4 | Prep: | Cook: 70mins | Ready in:

Ingredients

- 8 big potatoes unpeeled.
- For the cheese cream:
- 400 gr cheese cream.
- 1 c milk.
- 1 chili pepper.
- 1 medium onion chopped.
- 2 cloves garlic chopped.
- 1 gerkin chopped.
- 1 tbs green pepper chopped
- 4 tbs fresh herbs chopped (parsley,thyme,dill,mint) choose whatever you like.
- salt to taste.

Direction

- Wash and clean potatoes with a hard brush.
- Put potatoes in aluminium foil, bake in preheated oven on 200 C for air 180 C, 60-70 min.
- Set potatoes aside to cool.
- Cut chili in two and take seeds out and chop.
- Beat cream cheese with milk add onion, garlic, chili, green pepper, gherkin and herbs and salt to taste.
- Cut baked potatoes in halves
- Scoop flesh out (half egg deep).
- Add potato to cheese mixture and beat.
- Fill each half with cheese mixture.
- Serve the rest of the cheese mixture in a bowl separate.
- Serve with bread to dip.

123. Baked Spiraled Garlic Potatoes Recipe

Serving: 4 | Prep: | Cook: 60mins | Ready in:

Ingredients

- 4 baking potatoes,washed thoroughly
- 2 garlic cloves, cut into slivers
- 4 tablespoons ricotta cheese
- 4 tablespoon sour cream
- 2-3 tablespoons fresh chives, snipped

Direction

- Preheat the oven to 400 degrees.
- Slice each potato at about 1/4 inch intervals across, not cutting through to the base of the potato so that it keeps its shape.
- Slip the slivers of garlic between the cuts in the potatoes.
- Place the garlic filled potatoes in a roasting pan and bake 1-1 1/4 hours, or until soft when tested.
- Mix the ricotta cheese and sour cream in a bowl.
- Stir in the chopped chives.
- Serve the baked potatoes with a dollop of the cheese/sour cream mixture.
- These go great with grilled fish or meat!

124. Balsamic Baked Potatoes Recipe

Serving: 4 | Prep: | Cook: 80mins | Ready in:

Ingredients

- 1-1/2 lbs new potatoes,halved or quartered if large
- 3/4 c low-sodium chicken broth
- 1/4 c balsamic vinegar
- 8 glarlic cloves,smashed
- 5 sprigs thyme coarse salt and ground pepper

Direction

- Preheat oven to 425 degrees. In 8" square baking dish, combine potatoes, broth, vinegar, garlic and thyme; season with salt and pepper.
- Bake till potatoes are tender and liquid is reduced to a glaze, about 1-1/4 hours, tossing twice.

125. Beefy Spicy Baked Potatoes Recipe

Serving: 4 | Prep: | Cook: 60mins | Ready in:

Ingredients

- 4 baking potatoes
- 1 pound lean ground beef
- 12 ounce jar hot salsa
- 2 teaspoons chili powder
- 1/4 cup diced green bell pepper
- 1 tablespoon chopped stuffed green olives
- 1 cup shredded monterey jack cheese

Direction

- Scrub potatoes then pierce skin with fork and bake at 400 for 1 hour.
- Fifteen minutes before potatoes are done sauté beef in hot skillet until all pink disappears.
- Add salsa and chili powder to meat then cover and cook over medium for 10 minutes.
- Add green pepper and olives to meat mixture.
- Heat through.
- Cut baked potatoes open then spoon hot meat mixture into potatoes then top with cheese.

126. Best Simplest Baked Potato Recipe

Serving: 4 | Prep: | Cook: 75mins | Ready in:

Ingredients

- 4 idaho potatoes
- olive oil to coat
- salt (coarse preferred)
- fresh ground pepper
- garlic powder
- oregano

Direction

- Preheat oven to 350.
- Scrub potatoes until very clean.
- Dry, then using a standard fork poke 8 to 12 deep holes all over the spud so that moisture can escape during cooking.
- Coat in olive oil and season potatoes with salt, pepper, garlic powder and oregano.
- Place on a cookie sheet (DO NOT WRAP IN FOIL).
- Bake in oven for 1 hour and 15 mins or until skin feels crisp but flesh beneath feels soft.
- Serve by creating a dotted line from end to end with your fork, then crack the spud open by squeezing the ends towards one another. It will pop right open. But watch out, there will be some steam.
- I like them with some butter and scallions, but you can top them however you like.
- Don't be shy, you can eat the skin, it's so good for you, not to mention delicious!

127. Better Than Fries! Baked Potatoes Recipe

Serving: 1 | Prep: | Cook: 45mins | Ready in:

Ingredients

- Better than fries!
- Cut potatoes almost all the way through, drizzle olive oil, butter, salt & pepper over top & bake @425F for about 40 minutes.
- I have made these many times... using flavored cream cheese. Great Hit with all.

Direction

- Cutting them ahead and putting them in a zip lock bag with olive oil, makes the task of cutting not time consuming on the day of the big meal. Parsley sprinkles or grated cheeses add interest also.
- Can you tell I love these potatoes?

128. Boston Baked Potatoes Recipe

Serving: 1 | Prep: | Cook: 5mins | Ready in:

Ingredients

- russet potatoes

Direction

- Microwave potatoes about 5 min or till almost done.
- Cool a couple minutes until able to peel skin off.
- Deep fry at 375 degrees for about 5 minutes until golden brown.
- Drain on paper towel.
- Serve with sour cream, or French onion dip or just butter. Maybe ranch dressing

129. Broccoli Cheese Potato Bake Recipe

Serving: 8 | Prep: | Cook: 50mins | Ready in:

Ingredients

- 1 can Campbell's Condensed broccoli cheese soup
- 1/2 cup sour cream or yogurt
- 1/4 tsp. hot pepper sauce
- 7 small new potatoes, quartered
- 2 medium onions, cut into wedges
- 1/4 cup grated parmesan cheese

Direction

- In large bowl, combine soup, sour cream, and hot pepper sauce. Add potatoes and onions; toss to coat.
- In 2-quart baking dish, arrange potato mixture. Sprinkle with parmesan cheese. Bake at 375 degrees F. for 50 minutes or until potatoes are done.
- Makes 6 cups.

130. Brocoli And Bacon Baked Potato Recipe

Serving: 4 | Prep: | Cook: 60mins | Ready in:

Ingredients

- 4 medium russet potatoes, washed
- nonstick cooking spray
- kosher salt to taste
- 1/2 cup nonfat plain yogurt
- 1/2 cup broccoli florets, finely chopped
- 2 slices turkey bacon, crisply cooked and crumbled
- 20 cherry tomatoes, cut in half

Direction

- Preheat oven to 375F
- With a fork, poke 8 to 12 deep holes all over each potato so moisture can escape during cooking
- Place potatoes on a baking sheet and coat potatoes lightly with cooking spray
- Sprinkle with kosher salt and place baking sheet directly on rack in middle of oven
- Bake for 1 hour or until skin feels crisp but flesh beneath feels soft
- Remove from oven and let cool
- Once cool to the touch cut a slit down the middle of each potato

- Serve topped with a dollop of yogurt, some broccoli florets, crumbled bacon and halved cherry tomatoes

131. Buffalo Potatoes Recipe

Serving: 2 | Prep: | Cook: 15mins | Ready in:

Ingredients

- 2 baked potatoes sliced into 1/4" rounds
- 1 T butter
- 2-3 T hot sauce like Franks (Louisiana style)
- pinch garlic powder, thyme, lemon pepper,
- salt and pepper

Direction

- Over medium high heat melt the butter
- Add the potato rounds in a single layer
- Salt and pepper to taste
- When the down side is golden, turn
- Reseason with salt and pepper
- Whisk together the rest of the ingredients
- When both sides are golden, add the house sauce and toss.
- Serve immediately - Ranch dressing or sour cream make good dips

132. CARIBBEAN STYLE SPICY BAKED POTATOES Recipe

Serving: 4 | Prep: | Cook: 55mins | Ready in:

Ingredients

- 3 lbs. potatoes
- 4 onions, finely sliced
- 8 large ripe tomatoes, cubed
- 3 garlic cloves, minced
- 2 1/2 tsp. paprika powder
- 3 tbsp. cumin powder
- 1 1/2 cup meat or chicken broth (can be substituted by
- 1 1/2 cup of water and one condensed broth cube)
- 1 tbsp. wheat flour
- 3 tbsp. parsley, finely chopped
- 3 tbsp. olive or vegetable oil
- salt & pepper to taste

Direction

- Begin by boiling or baking the potatoes until halfway cooked but still somewhat firm. Let cool, then cut them in slices about 3/16" to 1/4" thick. You may leave the skin on.
- In the meanwhile, sauté the onions in the oil, adding the garlic a bit later and then adding the tomatoes, paprika, cumin, flour and broth and continue cooking, stirring regularly until a thick, chunky sauce in obtained.
- Add salt and pepper to your taste. In an oven-resistant transparent dish (or skillet), spread a very fine coating of the sauce, then divide the potatoes and the remaining sauce into three parts: place a layer of potatoes, sprinkle with a bit of salt (optional), cover it with a layer of sauce and sprinkle a tablespoon of parsley. Repeat 2 more times.
- Place the dish into a 350° preheated oven and cook until most of the boiling liquid is gone and a golden brownish colour is formed on its surface.
- A tasty dish for a light meal or as a side dish

133. Candied Baked Sweet Potato And Apples Recipe

Serving: 10 | Prep: | Cook: 30mins | Ready in:

Ingredients

- 1 tablespoon butter
- 2 Red Delicious apples; peeled, cored and sliced into rings

- 1 tablespoon lemon juice
- 1 28-oz can sweet potatoes; drained
- 1/4 cup brown sugar
- 1/4 teaspoon Apple spice Seasoning; See recipe
- 1/2 cup orange juice
- 1/4 cup dry sherry wine
- 3 tablespoons maraschino cherry juice
- 1/4 cup dark seedless raisins
- 1/4 cup light seedless raisins
- 1/2 cup pecan pieces
- 8 maraschino cherries

Direction

- Preheat oven to 350°F.
- Butter a shallow baking dish 8 X 11.5-inches.
- Drain the sweet potatoes and reserve the liquid in a small sauce pan.
- To the sweet potato liquid add the brown sugar, Apple Spice Seasoning, orange juice, sherry and Maraschino Cherry Juice.
- Heat to boiling and continue cooking to reduce the liquid to a thick syrup (soft candy stage).
- Remove the apple's cores and slice the apples into 3/8-inch cross section rings.
- Arrange on the bottom of the buttered baking dish. Drizzle on the lemon juice.
- Slice the drained sweet potatoes into 3/8-inch slices and arrange on and around the sliced apple rings.
- Sprinkle the dark and light raisins and pecans over the top of the sweet potatoes and apples.
- Arrange the Maraschino Cherries in the dish.
- Pour the candy syrup over the top of the fruit.
- Bake in a 350°F oven for 30 minutes.
- Allow to cool before serving.
- Note: An excellent condiment for Roast Turkey or Pork

134. Caramelized Onion Stuffed Baked Potatoes Recipe

Serving: 4 | Prep: | Cook: 15mins | Ready in:

Ingredients

- 2 medium baking potatoes (about 1 1/2 pounds)
- 1/2 c. (2 ounces) shredded Gruyère cheese, divided (or Swiss!)
- 2 TBSP. reduced-fat sour cream
- 1/2 tsp. salt
- 1/4 tsp. freshly ground black pepper
- 1 1/2 tsp. butter
- 2 c. vertically sliced red onion
- 2 tsp. sugar
- 2 TBSP. dry sherry, optional
- 1 tsp. worcestershire sauce
- 1/2 tsp. dried thyme
- 1 garlic clove, minced

Direction

- Pierce potatoes with a fork; arrange on paper towels in microwave oven. Microwave at high 10 minutes or until done, rearranging potatoes after 5 minutes. Let stand 5 minutes.
- Cut each potato in half lengthwise; scoop out pulp, leaving a 1/4-inch-thick shell. Combine potato pulp, 1/4 cup cheese, sour cream, salt, and pepper. Spoon potato mixture evenly into shells.
- Melt butter in a medium non-stick skillet over medium-high heat. Add onion and sugar; sauté 8 minutes or until browned. Stir in sherry, Worcestershire, thyme, and garlic; cook 1 minute or until liquid evaporates, scraping pan to loosen browned bits. Top each potato half with about 2 tablespoons onion mixture and 1 tablespoon of cheese. Arrange stuffed potato halves on paper towels in microwave oven. Microwave at high 1 minute or until thoroughly heated.

135. Cheddar Baked Potato Slices Recipe

Serving: 6 | Prep: | Cook: 55mins | Ready in:

Ingredients

- 1 can (10 3/4 oz.) Campbell's Cream of Mushroom Soup
- 1/2 tsp. paprika
- 1/2 tsp. black pepper
- 4 medium baking potatoes, cut into 1/4 inch slices (about 4 cups)
- 1 cup shredded cheddar cheese

Direction

- In small bowl, combine soup, paprika and pepper.
- In greased 2 qt. baking dish, arrange potatoes in overlapping rows.
- Sprinkle with cheese.
- Spoon soup mixture over cheese.
- Cover with foil.
- Bake at 400 degrees for 45 minutes.
- Uncover and bake 10 minutes or until potatoes are fork tender.

136. Cheddar Potato Bake Recipe

Serving: 8 | Prep: | Cook: 35mins | Ready in:

Ingredients

- Cheddar potato Bake
- 1 can (103/4 oz.) condensed cheddar cheese soup
- 1/3 cup sour cream or plain yogurt
- 4 TBS. Chopped green onions,
- black pepper to taste
- 3 cups stiff seasoned mashed potatoes
- 1/2 cup shredded cheddar cheese
- 2 TBS. dry bread crumbs
- 1 TBS. margarine or butter, melted
- ¼ tsp. paprika

Direction

- Preheat oven to 350
- In a 1/1/2 quart casserole dish, combine soup, sour cream, half of the onions, and pepper.
- Stir in potatoes until blended.
- In a small bowl, combine bread crumbs, butter, and paprika. Sprinkle evenly over potatoes.
- Bake at 350 for 30 minutes or until hot and bubbling. Garnish with shredded cheese and pop back in oven for 5 minutes to allow cheese to melt. Garnish with other half of green onions.

137. Cheese Potato And Onion Bake Recipe

Serving: 6 | Prep: | Cook: 50mins | Ready in:

Ingredients

- 8 red potatoes, sliced
- 2 large sweet onions, sliced
- 1/2 C butter, sliced
- 1 C shredded cheddar cheese
- 1/4 tsp garlic salt
- salt and pepper to taste

Direction

- Place potatoes, onions, butter and garlic salt together in a large greased baking dish.
- Sprinkle with salt and pepper.
- Cover casserole dish with aluminum foil.
- Preheat oven to 350 degrees.
- Bake casserole for 40 minutes or until potatoes are fork tender.
- Stir occasionally.
- Remove casserole from oven and sprinkle top with cheese.
- Bake uncovered for 10 minutes or until cheese completely melts.

138. Cheese Sauced Baked Potatoes Recipe

Serving: 6 | Prep: | Cook: 50mins | Ready in:

Ingredients

- 6 baking potatoes, your favorite variety
- 1 cup shredded sharp cheddar cheese
- 1/2 cup sour cream
- 1/2 stick butter
- 2 Tbsp chopped green onion

Direction

- Set out cheese, sour cream, butter and onion so they can come to room temperature.
- Scrub potatoes thoroughly. Prick potatoes with tines of fork.
- Bake at 425 for 40 to 60 minutes or until done.
- Before potatoes are done, combine cheese, sour cream, butter and onion in a small bowl and beat them until they are fluffy.
- Pick up hot potatoes with pot holders or oven mitts and roll gently between the palms of your hands.
- Cut a crisscross in top of each potato and press the ends so that the centres fluff up.
- Spoon cheese topping over each potato.

139. Cheesy Baked Potato Surprise Recipe

Serving: 6 | Prep: | Cook: 30mins | Ready in:

Ingredients

- 8 medium potatoes, peeled and sliced
- 2 large onions
- 4 TBSP butter, divided
- 16 ounces of fresh sliced mushrooms
- 2 cups small curd cottage cheese.
- 1/2 cup sour cream
- 2 cups shredded cheddar cheese divided
- 2 tsp dried thyme
- 2 tsp. salt
- 1 tsp. black pepper

Direction

- Place potatoes in pan of hot water and boil just until tender, drain.
- Sauté onions in 2 TBSP butter. Remove onions leave the butter in the pan and sauté mushrooms. Drain mushrooms.
- Preheat oven to 350 degrees. Spray a 13x9 inch baking dish with Pam.
- Combine cottage cheese, sour cream, and 1 1/2 cups of cheese in bowl.
- Layer potatoes, onions, mushrooms, and cottage cheese mixture in baking dish. Sprinkle each layer with thyme, salt and pepper. Sprinkle remaining cheese on top of potatoes. Bake about 30 minutes.

140. Chicken & Potato Bake Recipe

Serving: 0 | Prep: | Cook: 2hours | Ready in:

Ingredients

- 2 1/2 to 3# frying chicken pieces skins removed (optional)
- 3 large potatoes cut into wedges
- 2 medium onions, diced
- 1 1/2 tsp. garlic salt
- 1/4 tsp. pepper
- 2 (14 1/2-oz) diced tomatoes (drained)
- 1/4 cup chopped parsley

Direction

- Preheat oven to 350 degrees
- Place chicken pieces in a 13x9x2 inch baking dish

- Arrange potatoes over chicken; top with onion
- Sprinkle garlic salt & pepper evenly over onion
- Spoon tomatoes over dish & top with parsley
- Cover with foil & bake @ 350 degrees for 1 1/2 hr. or until
- Chicken is no longer pink in the centre & potatoes are tender

- Mix enchilada sauce, soup and green chilies in a bowl
- Pour mixture over all ingredients to cover
- Bake at 350 degrees for 45 mins. uncovered
- Remove and top with shredded Mexican blend cheese
- Cook another 10 to 15 minutes
- Remove, let cool for 5 minutes, plate and enter heaven

141. Chicken Potato Enchilada Bake Recipe

Serving: 6 | Prep: | Cook: 60mins | Ready in:

Ingredients

- one pound cooked cubed chicken breast
- frozen hash brown patties
- 28 oz can mild to hot enchilada sauce
- 10 oz can Campbell's Southwest pepper Jack soup
- 4 oz can of fire roasted diced green chilis
- 16 oz can fat free jalapeno refried beans
- 4 oz sliced fresh mozzerella cheese
- 1 cup shredded sharp cheddar cheese
- one half cup finely shredded Mexican blend cheese
- vegetable oil
- 1 cup chopped onion

Direction

- Pour enough oil into 13X9 baking dish to cover bottom to just coat
- Add layer of hash brown patties to cover bottom
- Spread chicken evenly over patties
- Sprinkle onion over chicken
- Sprinkle with cheddar cheese
- Spread layer of refried beans after heating to soften
- Evenly place sliced mozzarella cheese on beans

142. Chicken Sausage And Potato Bake Recipe

Serving: 6 | Prep: | Cook: 75mins | Ready in:

Ingredients

- 3 lbs skinless, boneless chicken pieces
- 1 lb Italian-style sausage (mild or spicy, as you like it)
- 6 potatoes
- 1 medium onion, chopped
- 1/2 lb mushrooms, cleaned and chopped
- 1/3 cup olive oil
- 2 teaspoons oregano
- 1 teaspoon rosemary
- 1/2 teaspoon freshly ground black pepper
- 2 teaspoons paprika (you may use less if the sausage is spicy)
- 1 teaspoon garlic salt
- 4 tablespoons dried parsley

Direction

- Mix all the spices together in a small dish and set aside.
- Peel and cut the potatoes in bite-sized pieces and place them in the bottom of a baking pot.
- Sprinkle about 1/3 of the combined spices over the potatoes.
- Layer the onions and mushrooms on top of the potatoes.
- Layer the chicken pieces on top of the vegetables.

- Lay the sausage, cut into bite-sized pieces, atop the chicken.
- Sprinkle the remaining blended spices on top of everything.
- Sprinkle the olive oil over the entire pot.
- Place in a pre-heated 425-degree F oven for 30 minutes.
- Reduce the oven heat to 375-degrees and bake for 45 more minutes, until the potatoes are cooked and the sausage is browned.

143. Chili Baked Potato Recipe

Serving: 4 | Prep: | Cook: 15mins | Ready in:

Ingredients

- 4 medium potatoes, cut in half
- 1 can chili, with or without beans
- seasonings, to taste
- sour cream
- salsa
- cheddar
- chopped green onions

Direction

- Split potatoes and poke with a fork. Microwave until cooked, (about 12 minutes). Squeeze potatoes to soften the insides. Top each potato with heated chili, sour cream, salsa, cheddar cheese and green onions.

144. Chilli Seasoned Potato Wedges Recipe

Serving: 0 | Prep: | Cook: 49mins | Ready in:

Ingredients

- 1 tablespoon onion soup mix
- 1 tablespoon chili powder
- 1/4 teaspoon salt
- 1/4 teaspoon garlic powder
- 1/4 teaspoon pepper
- 4 large baking potatoes
- 2 tablespoons vegetable oil

Direction

- 1. In a large resealable plastic bag, combine soup mix, chilli powder, salt, garlic powder and pepper.
- 2. Cut each potato into eight wedges, place in bag and shake to coat.
- 3. Arrange in a single layer in a greased 15 in x 10 in x 1 in baking pan. Drizzle with oil.
- 4. Bake uncovered at 425 for 20 minutes.
- 5. Turn bake 15-20 minutes longer or until crisp.

145. Chive And Garlic Potato Bake Recipe

Serving: 2 | Prep: | Cook: 5mins | Ready in:

Ingredients

- 2 Medium potatoes
- 1/2 cup Grated cheese
- 4 tsp butter
- 1/2 tub of garlic chive Dip
- 4 pickled onions
- Sprinkle of Parmesan
- 3 stalks parsley

Direction

- Steam potatoes.
- Place on aluminium foil and break apart into a pile.
- Spread dip, butter and sliced pickled onions over potatoes.
- Sprinkle cheese over and season.
- Sprinkle parmesan over the top.
- Place under griller until brown.

- Sprinkle with chopped parsley.

---

146. Chorizo And Cheese Baked Potatoes Recipe

Serving: 8 | Prep: | Cook: 60mins | Ready in:

Ingredients

- 1 egg
- 2 tbls. lemon juice
- 1/2 tsp. dry mustard
- 1/2 tsp. salt
- 1 cup olive oil
- 1 lb. velveeta
- 1/2 lb. chorizo, cut into 1/4 inch cubes
- 4 jalapenos, seeded and chopped
- 8 baked potatoes

Direction

- In blender, add egg, lemon juice, mustard and salt
- Blend well
- Gradually add oil until mixture is the consistency of mayonnaise
- In saucepan, melt cheese over very low heat
- Add egg mixture, chorizo, and jalapenos, and stir until blended
- Serve over baked potato

---

147. Clam And Potato Bake Recipe

Serving: 2 | Prep: | Cook: 45mins | Ready in:

Ingredients

- 8 medium red potatoes, scrubbed
- 1 pound clams in shell, scrubbed
- 1 pound mussels, cleaned and debearded
- 1/2 pound unpeeled large shrimp
- 1 (48 fluid ounce) can chicken broth
- 1/4 cup dry vermouth (optional)
- 3/4 cup butter, divided
- 1 loaf French bread

Direction

- Place a potatoes in a layer in the bottom of a large pot. Cover with a layer of clams, then mussels, and finally the shrimp. Pour in the vermouth and enough chicken broth to fill the pot halfway. You may not need all of the broth, depending on the size of your pot. Cut half of the butter into cubes and place on top of the seafood. Cover with a lid, and seal tightly with aluminum foil
- Bring to a boil, then simmer over medium-low heat for 45 minutes. Remove from the heat, and carefully remove the foil and lid. Remove the seafood and potatoes from the liquid to serve. Melt 1/2 remaining butter, and divide into 4 individual dishes for dipping. Serve with the rest of the butter and French bread.

---

148. Colcannon Stuffed Baked Potatoes Recipe

Serving: 4 | Prep: | Cook: 90mins | Ready in:

Ingredients

- 4 large baking potatoes
- 3 cups shredded green gcabbage, 3/8" shreds
- 1/2 cup onion, chpped finely
- 1 Tbl. oil
- 1 Tbl. soy sauce
- 1/2 tsp. dill seed
- 2 Tbl. butter
- 1 tsp. lemon juice
- 1/4 tsp. salt
- 1/4 tsp. pepper
- 3-4 Tbl. cream
- sour cream, to top (optional)
- Fresh snipped dill or chives (optional)

Direction

- Clean potatoes and dry.
- Prick skins with a fork.
- Bake the potatoes in a 425 degree oven for 1 hour or until tender.
- Meanwhile, in a medium sauce pan cook the cabbage and onion in hot oil for 5 minutes.
- Add water, soy sauce, and dill seed: bring to a boil.
- Lower heat and simmer, covered, for about 10 minutes.
- Cut a thin lengthwise slice off the top of each potato.
- Using a spoon, gently scoop out the pulp leaving a 1/4" thick shell.
- In a bowl mash the potato pulp, stirring in the butter, lemon juice, salt and pepper.
- Stir in the cabbage mixture.
- Adjust consistency with cream (should be creamy, not loose).
- Spoon the mixture back into the potato shells, and place in a shallow baking pan.
- Bake at 425 degrees for 15 minutes or until heated through.
- To serve, top with sour cream and snipped dill or chives if desired.

149. Country Potato Pancakes

Serving: 0 | Prep: | Cook: | Ready in:

Ingredients

- 3 large potatoes (about 2 pounds), peeled
- 2 large eggs, lightly beaten
- 1 tablespoon grated onion
- 2 tablespoons all-purpose flour
- 1 teaspoon salt
- 1/2 teaspoon baking powder
- Vegetable oil for frying

Direction

- Finely grate potatoes. Drain any liquid. Add eggs, onion, flour, salt and baking powder. In a frying pan, add oil to the depth of 1/8 in.; heat over medium-high (375°).
- Drop batter by heaping tablespoonfuls in hot oil. Flatten into patties. Fry until golden brown, turning once. Serve immediately.
- Tips:
- Warm leftover pancakes in the oven and have them with breakfast. Serve as a snack with smoked salmon or applesauce.
- Have these latkes as part of your Hanukkah celebration—along with these other traditional recipes.
- Nutrition Facts
- 2 pancakes: 257 calories, 8g fat (1g saturated fat), 31mg cholesterol, 242mg sodium, 41g carbohydrate (2g sugars, 5g fiber), 6g protein.

150. Country Style Potato Bake Recipe

Serving: 8 | Prep: | Cook: 15mins | Ready in:

Ingredients

- 1 kg potatoes
- 1/2 - 3/4 cup of thickened cream
- 1-2 garlic cloves (to preferance)
- 5 rashers bacon, only middle not ends; too fatty
- 1 cup grated tasty cheese

Direction

- Peel and cube potatoes to about 1.5cm
- Place in microwave safe dish with small amount of water, microwave on high for 6 min stirring once or until potatoes are tender.
- Roughly chop bacon
- Crush fresh garlic into cream
- Add potatoes to oven proof dish
- Add bacon, cream and cover with cheese
- Bake uncovered for 10 min or until cheese is melted

151. Creamy Baked Potatoes Recipe

Serving: 6 | Prep: | Cook: 60mins | Ready in:

Ingredients

- 3 cups diced cooked potatoes
- 1 cup cream of mushroom soup
- 1/2 cup cooked mushrooms
- 8 ounces sour cream
- 1 cup grated cheddar cheese
- 1/4 cup diced onion
- 2 tablespoons butter

Direction

- Mix soup, sour cream, mushrooms, onions and cheese then fold in potatoes and pour into shallow baking dish.
- Dot with butter and bake at 350 for 1 hour.

152. Creamy Mashed Potato Bake Recipe

Serving: 6 | Prep: | Cook: 30mins | Ready in:

Ingredients

- 3 cups mashed potatoes
- 1 cup sour cream
- 1/4 cup milk
- 1/4 tsp garlic powder
- 1 1/3 cups French fried onions
- 1 cup shredded cheddar cheese

Direction

- Combine mashed potatoes, sour cream, milk, and garlic powder.
- Spoon half the mixture into 2 quart casserole. Sprinkle with 2/3 cup fried onions and 1/2 cup cheese. Top with remaining potato mixture.
- Bake 30 minutes at 350 degrees or until hot. Top with remaining onions and cheese. Bake 5 minutes

153. Creamy Potato Bake Recipe

Serving: 6 | Prep: | Cook: 30mins | Ready in:

Ingredients

- 6 servings instant mashed potatoes
- 1 4-ounce carton whipped cream cheese
- 1 beaten egg
- 2 tablespoons finely chopped grean onion
- 1 tablespoon finely snipped parsley
- paprika

Direction

- Prepare 6 servings instant mashed potatoes using package directions, omitting the butter.
- Add one 4-ounce carton whipped cream cheese; beat well.
- Stir in 1 beaten egg, 2 tablespoons finely chopped green onion, and 1 tablespoon finely snipped parsley; blend well.
- Transfer to a well-greased 1-quart baking dish.
- Dot with 1 tablespoon butter.
- Sprinkle with paprika.
- Bake at 400 for 30 minutes.
- Serves 6.

154. Creamy Potato Gratin With Attitude Recipe

Serving: 12 | Prep: | Cook: 30mins | Ready in:

Ingredients

- 4 1/2 pounds all-purpose potatoes
- 2 cups whole milk
- 2 cups heavy cream
- 1 onion, julianned
- 2 cloves garlic, minced
- 1-2 jalapenos minced
- 1 tablespoon salt
- olive oil for saute
- Approximately 1/4 cup unsalted butter
- 1 cup Parmasian cheese
- 1/2 cup Fontina cheese
- 1/2 cup of smoked Gouda cheese

Direction

- Preheat the oven to 500 degrees F.
- Peel the potatoes and cut them into slices, neither especially thin nor especially thick (approximately 1/2-inch) and put them into a large saucepan with the milk, cream, and salt. Bring to the boil and cook at a robust simmer or gentle boil (however you like to think of it) until verging on tender, but not dissolving into mush.
- Sauté the onions garlic and jalapenos in olive oil until translucent then add to the potato mixture.
- The pan might be hell to clean afterward, but any excuse for long, lazy soaking rather than brisk pre-or postprandial scrubbing always appeals to me. And, for what it's worth, I find that when pans are really, dauntingly, stuck with cooked-on gunge, it's more effective to soak them in hot water and detergent
- Use some of the butter to grease a large roasting pan (15 by 12-inches) and then pour the almost sludgy milk and potato mixture into it. Add Gouda, Fontina, and parmesan cheese by spreading evenly over potatoes then gently folding into the mix. Dot with remaining butter and cook in the oven for 15 - 20 minutes or until the potato is bubbly and browned on top. Remove, let stand for 10 to 20 minutes and then serve.
- This is not the most labour saving way of cooking potatoes, to be sure, but one of the most seductive. And it reheats well as an accompaniment to cold roast pork, or indeed anything in the days that follow.

155. Creamy Red Potatoes Recipe

Serving: 8 | Prep: | Cook: 6hours5mins | Ready in:

Ingredients

- 2 1/2 lbs. red potatoes, washed and cut into 1/2 inch cubes
- Sauce
- 8 oz package cream cheese, softened
- 10 3/4 oz can of cream of potato soup
- 1 envelope dry rance dressing mix
- 4 tbsp. milk

Direction

- Beat sauce ingredients together. Stir in potatoes in crock pot. Cook on LOW for 5-6 hours.
- To do these in the oven, pre-cook the potatoes for 5 to 10 minutes. Drain. Make sauce and add to potatoes. Spoon into a 9x13 inch glass pan. Bake at 350* until hot about 35-45 minutes.

156. Crispy Baked Potato Wedges With Cajun Aioli Recipe

Serving: 4 | Prep: | Cook: 30mins | Ready in:

Ingredients

- 2 large idaho potatoes, peeled and sliced into long wedges
- olive oil
- cajun spice Mix (I used one in bag from Cost Plus Imports or you can make your own)
- kosher salt

- Cajun Aioli:
- 1/2 cup Best Food mayonaise
- cajun spice mix, to taste
- about a TBSP fresh lemon juice
- a little chopped parsley

Direction

- Mix all the ingredients for the Cajun aioli and keep in refrigerator until ready to serve.
- Preheat oven to 400 degrees F.
- Place the potato wedges in a saucepan with 2 quarts of cold salted water. Bring to a boil and then reduce to a simmer for approximately 5 minutes, or until a knife pierces through easily. Drain.
- In a large bowl, toss the wedges with olive oil. Place the wedges on a baking sheet lined with parchment in single layer. Sprinkle with Cajun spice and salt. Bake for 20-30 minutes, or until golden brown crispy.
- Sprinkle with fresh chopped parsley and serve with Cajun Aioli

157. Crispy Crust Baked Potatoes Recipe

Serving: 4 | Prep: | Cook: 50mins | Ready in:

Ingredients

- 4 6-8 oz long baking potatoes, peeled.
- 3 Tbsp extra-virgin olive oil, divided
- 1/4 cup parmesan cheese
- 1/2 cup fine breadcrumps
- 1tsp paprika
- kosher salt to taste
- 2 Tbsp melted butter
- 2 tsp fresh parsley, minced for garnish

Direction

- Place the potatoes in cold water to prevent browning as they are prepared.
- Cut and discard a thin lengthwise slice from the bottom of each potato so that they will sit flat on a cutting board.
- Place two long handled wooden spoons or chopsticks lengthwise on both sides of potato to prevent knife from cutting entirely through. Using a sharp knife held at right angles to the wooden spoons or chopsticks, thinly slice potatoes crosswise, do not cut completely through.
- Return potatoes to cold water and repeat this process until all potatoes are sliced.
- Towel dry potatoes, place cut side up in a shallow greased baking pan, brush with 1 tablespoons oil.
- In a food processor puree the Parmesan cheese, breadcrumbs, paprika, salt and remaining 2 tablespoon extra-virgin olive oil; spread on potatoes pressing to adhere. Cover with foil and bake potatoes at 450° for 30 minutes. Remove foil and bake 15-20 minutes more.
- The potato slices fan out as they bake. Drizzle with melted butter, parsley and serve.

158. Crockpot Baked Potato Recipe

Serving: 0 | Prep: | Cook: 10hours9mins | Ready in:

Ingredients

- 6-8 potatoes
- 1 ounce olive oil
- Tin foil

Direction

- Prick potatoes with a fork.
- *opt. rub with Olive oil
- Wrap well in foil.
- Place in crockpot. Cover; cook on low for 8-10 hours.

159. Crump Topped Sour Cream Cheesy Potato Bake Recipe

Serving: 6 | Prep: | Cook: 30mins | Ready in:

Ingredients

- 1 can cheddar cheese soup
- 1/3 cup sour cream
- 2 tablespoons chopped green onions
- 1 tablespoon freshly ground black pepper
- 3 cups seasoned mashed potatoes
- 1 tablespoon melted butter
- 2 tablespoons dry breadcrumbs
- 1/4 teaspoon paprika
- 1/4 teaspoon cayenne pepper

Direction

- Combine soup, sour cream, green onions and pepper.
- Mix well and stir in potatoes then place in casserole.
- Mix butter, breadcrumbs, paprika and cayenne pepper then pour over potato mixture.
- Bake at 350 for 30 minutes.

160. Crunchy Blue Cheese And Walnut Filled Baked Potatoes Recipe

Serving: 4 | Prep: | Cook: 15mins | Ready in:

Ingredients

- 4 large baking potatoes
- 1 apple, sliced
- lemon juice
- 2 stalks celery, sliced
- 1/4 cup walnuts, chopped
- 150 grs Greek yogurt
- 50 grs blue cheese
- salt and pepper

Direction

- Bake the potatoes as usual (I normally microwave them on full, hence the 15 minutes).
- In the meantime, sprinkle the sliced apple with lemon juice to prevent discoloration.
- Put the celery, apple and walnuts in a bowl and add the yogurt.
- Crumble the blue cheese into the bowl, then toss all the ingredients together until well combined.
- When the potatoes are ready, cut a cross in the top of each one.
- Gently squeeze each potato to open out the cross slightly.
- Season the potatoes with salt and pepper.
- Spoon the blue cheese mixture on top.
- Enjoy!

161. DOUBLE BAKED STUFFED POTATOES Recipe

Serving: 10 | Prep: | Cook: 60mins | Ready in:

Ingredients

- 5 LRG BAKING potatoS
- 1 CUP heavy whipping cream
- 3/4 CUP butter
- 2-4 CUPS SHREDDED cheddar cheese
- crab TO TASTE

Direction

- BAKE POTATOS AT 400 DEGREES FOR 45 MINUTES
- REMOVE FROM OVEN TO PARTIALLY COOL
- IN A MEDIUM BOIL BLEND REMAINING INGREDIENTS, SET ASIDE
- CAREFULLY SPLIT AND SCOOP OUT CENTER OF POTATOS

- MASH THE POTATO CENTERS
- ADD CHEESE MIXTURE
- STUFF POTATO SKINS
- BAKE AT 200 DEGREES FOR 15 MINUTES

162. Damn Hot Peppers With Potato Hash With Baked Eggs Recipe

Serving: 4 | Prep: | Cook: 30mins | Ready in:

Ingredients

- 2 large russet potatoes, peeled and cut into 1/2-inch dice
- 1/4 cup extra-virgin olive oil
- 1/4 cup chopped onion
- sea salt, preferably gray salt
- Freshly ground black pepper
- 1 1/2 cups Damn hot peppers, at room temperature
- 4 eggs
- 1 teaspoon chopped fresh oregano
- 3 tablespoons freshly grated Parmesan, Asiago, or other aged cheese

Direction

- Preheat the oven to 375°F.
- Bring a pot of well-salted water to a boil.
- Add the potatoes and boil until about three-quarters done, about 4 minutes.
- Drain well.
- Heat a large ovenproof skillet over high heat.
- When hot, add the olive oil, then add the potatoes.
- Lower the heat to medium and cook, tossing occasionally, until the potatoes are crusty and browned, 10 to 12 minutes.
- Add the onion, season with salt and pepper, and cook until the onion browns lightly, about 2 minutes.
- Drain the potatoes and onion in a sieve to remove the excess oil, then return them to the skillet.
- Off the heat, gently stir in the Damn Hot Peppers.
- If you blend them in too well, the potatoes will lose their crispness. Make 4 evenly spaced wells in the hash and break an egg into each well.
- Sprinkle the eggs with the oregano and scatter the cheese over the hash.
- Transfer the skillet to the oven and bake until the eggs are cooked to your taste, about 6 minutes for firm whites and soft yolks. Serve immediately.
- Michael's Tips: Boiling the potatoes first helps keep them from sticking to the skillet. So does preheating the pan until it's hot, hot, hot. Don't be afraid of a hot skillet. That's how chefs get such beautifully browned surfaces on foods.

163. Delicious Chicken Bake With Potato Crust Recipe

Serving: 6 | Prep: | Cook: 30mins | Ready in:

Ingredients

- 3 cups mashed hot potato
- 1 cup shredded cheddar cheese
- 2.8 oz french fried onions
- 1 1/2 cups cubed cooked chicken
- 1 pkge.(10oz) frozen veggies (any you really want-I use mixed veggies)
- 1 can condensed cream of chicken soup
- 1/4 cup milk
- 1/2 tsp ground mustard
- 1/4 tsp garlic powder
- salt and pepper to taste

Direction

- Preheat oven to 375

- In a medium bowl combine mashed potatoes, 1/2 cup cheese and 1/2 the can of the French fried onions; mix well
- Spoon potato mixture into a greased casserole dish. Spread up sides to make a nice potato shell. (Do not use a long casserole dish)
- In a large bowl, combine chicken, mixed veggies, soup, milk and spices
- Pour into the shell
- Bake uncovered, at 375 for 30 minutes... until nice and bubbly
- Top with remaining cheese and French fried onions
- Bake, uncovered for 3 or so minutes until nice and brown

164. Dijon Baked Potatoes With Cheese And Bacon Aka Twice Baked Recipe

Serving: 4 | Prep: | Cook: 50mins | Ready in:

Ingredients

- 4 large baking potatoes, rubbed with olive oil, pierced and baked in a 400 degree oven for about 50 minutes
- 1 cup shredded Jack or sharp cheddar cheese
- 1/2 cup sour cream
- 4 slices cooked bacon or ham, chopped
- 4 green onions, chopped
- 2 t Dijon mustard
- 1/2-1 t hot red pepper sauce
- chives for topping
- Note: Substitute low fat cheese and sour cream and lean ham for a healthier version-- still good!

Direction

- Allow potatoes to cool a bit and cut a slit in the top of each
- Squeeze the potato open and scrape out the filling, leaving about a 1/2 shell
- It is fine to remove the top of the potato lengthwise to get to the pulp (like making a boat or canoe)
- Mix the cooked pulp with the cheese mixture
- Mound the filling into the potato shells
- Place the stuffed potatoes into a greased baking dish
- Bake about 15 minutes or until the cheese is melted
- Sprinkle with chives
- Enjoy

165. Double Baked Mashed Potatoes With Fontina And Italian Parsley Recipe

Serving: 4 | Prep: | Cook: 90mins | Ready in:

Ingredients

- INGREDIENTS
- 2 pounds medium-size russet potatoes
- 3/4 cup half and half
- 2 tablespoons (1/4 stick) butter
- 1 and 1/4 cups (packed) grated Fontina cheese (about 6 ounces)
- 3 tablespoons chopped fresh Italian parsley
- salt and pepper to taste
- chopped scallions for garnish

Direction

- DIRECTIONS:
- Preheat oven to 375°F.
- Using small knife, pierce potatoes in several places.
- Place potatoes on small baking sheet.
- Bake until tender when pierced with skewer, about 1 hour. Cool slightly.
- Bring half and half to simmer in heavy small saucepan.
- Scrape potatoes from skin into large bowl.
- Using ricer, food mill or potato masher, mash potatoes.

- Mix in half and half.
- Add butter; stir vigorously until butter melts and potatoes are smooth.
- Stir in 2/3 of cheese and 3 tablespoons parsley.
- Season with salt and pepper.
- Transfer potatoes to 11 x 7 x 2-inch glass baking dish.
- Sprinkle with remaining cheese. Some finely chopped chives would be pretty on top.
- Can be prepared 2 hours ahead. Cover and let stand at room temperature.
- Preheat oven to 425°F.
- Bake potatoes until heated through and cheese melts, about 15 minutes.
- Let's eat!

166. Double Baked Potato With Low Fat Yogurt And Crispy Onions Recipe

Serving: 8 | Prep: | Cook: 90mins | Ready in:

Ingredients

- 4 large potatoes, scrubbed, but with skin still intact
- 1 cup kosher salt
- 1 cup low fat plain yogurt
- 3 tablespoons olive oil
- 1 large sweet onion, thinly sliced
- salt and pepper to taste

Direction

- Preheat oven to 400°F. Pierce the potatoes with a fork in several places. Place the kosher salt in a roasting pan, lay potatoes on top and bake until fully cooked, about one hour. Remove potatoes from the oven and allow to cool until you can handle them.
- Cut the potatoes in half lengthwise and scoop out the potato pulp into a bowl, leaving about 1/4-inch of pulp all around to form a potato "shell." Combine the potato pulp and yogurt, using a fork to mash together.
- Brush the potato skins with one tablespoon olive oil and place them back into the oven to continue to cook until crispy, about 20 minutes. Meanwhile, sauté the onions in the remaining olive oil over very low heat until well browned and caramelized, about 15 minutes. Add cooked onions to the potato pulp mixture; season with salt and pepper.
- When potato skins are done, remove them from the oven and spoon the pulp mixture into the skins, dividing up the mixture evenly. Return potatoes to the oven again and bake for an additional 10 minutes before serving.

167. Double Baked Sardine Potatoes Recipe

Serving: 2 | Prep: | Cook: 50mins | Ready in:

Ingredients

- 6 red potatoes
- 2 spigs rosemary, chopped
- olive or vegetable oil
- basil or parsley flakes
- 2 sardines, mashed
- 1 red chilli, de-seeded, chopped
- 1/2 medium onion, diced
- salt & pepper
- 1 lime, squeezed

Direction

- Mix the sardine, chilli, onion, salt, pepper & lime juice in a bowl (mixture 1). Set aside.
- Wash and scrub potatoes. Use a fork and poke all over the potatoes.
- Coat the potatoes evenly with oil (this makes the skin crisper after baking).
- Bake the potatoes in preheated oven (200C, 400F) for 50 minutes, or till soft (use a fork to test).

- Cut the cooked potatoes in halves and scoop out the flesh using a spoon or melon ball scooper.
- Mix the chopped rosemary and potatoes' flesh in a bowl and then combine thoroughly with mixture 1 using a fork.
- Transfer the entire mixture back to the individual potato shells and top with basil or parsley flakes. Bake for another 5 minutes. Serve.

168. Easter Mashed Baked Potatos Recipe

Serving: 10 | Prep: | Cook: 45mins | Ready in:

Ingredients

- 4 Cups frozen hash browns
- 1 (7.6-ounce) package butter and herb mashed potato mix. (I used two 4 oz. Idahoan butter & herb.)
- 1 stick butter, softened
- 4 ounces cream cheese, softened
- 1 cup shredded monterey jack cheese
- 1/2 cup sour cream
- 1/2 teaspoon garlic salt
- 1/2 teaspoon salt
- 1/2 teaspoon pepper
- 2 cups boiling water
- 2 cups prepared french-fred onion rings
- Preheat oven to 350 degrees F.

Direction

- Bring a pot of water to boiling, and add the hash browns. Cook for five minutes and drain. In a large bowl, mix together the cooked hash browns, mashed potato mix, butter, cream cheese, jack cheese, sour cream, garlic salt, salt and pepper. Stir in the boiling water. Place in a greased 2-quart casserole dish.
- Bake for 35 to 45 minutes. Sprinkle the onion rings over the casserole and bake for about 5 to 8 minutes longer until onions are golden brown.

169. Easy Baked Chicken Potatoes And Carrots Recipe

Serving: 0 | Prep: | Cook: | Ready in:

Ingredients

- 1 Reynolds Oven Bag, large
- 1 tablespoon flour
- 1 whole chicken
- bunch of baby carrots
- 4 potatoes peeled and cut in half
- salt to taste
- lemon pepper
- paprika

Direction

- Preheat oven to 350 degrees F.
- Shake flour in cooking bag; place in 13x9x2-inch pan.
- Place chicken in cooking bag.
- Add potatoes and carrots.
- Sprinkle with the lemon pepper, paprika and salt.
- Close oven bag with nylon tie, cut six 1/2-inch slits in top.
- Bake until chicken is tender and potatoes and carrots are cooked, about 1 1/2 hours.

170. Easy Cheesy Potatoes Recipe

Serving: 4 | Prep: | Cook: 1hours | Ready in:

Ingredients

- 8 med potatoes
- 1 cup shredded cheddar cheese

- 1 can cream of mushroom soup

Direction

- Wash, peel and slice potatoes.
- Mix all ingredients together.
- Bake at 350 for 1 hr. or until top starts to brown.

171. Ever So Slightly Sweet Potato Cashew Bake Recipe

Serving: 8 | Prep: | Cook: 45mins | Ready in:

Ingredients

- 6 medium sweet potatoes
- 2 tablespoons brown sugar mixed with 1 teaspoon ground ginger
- 4 tablespoons butter (use the real thing, please!)
- 1/2 cup broken cashews
- kosher salt

Direction

- Scrub and peel sweet potatoes, then cut into chunks.
- Place sweet potatoes in pot and cover with water.
- Parboil until just tender (approximately 15 minutes)
- Remove from heat and drain.
- Layer sweet potatoes in a greased casserole dish.
- Dot with butter.
- Sprinkle with brown sugar-ginger mix.
- Add a pinch of kosher salt.
- Dust lightly with my Signature Spice Blend (optional)
- Bake, in a 350 oven, covered for about 20 minutes.
- Uncover and sprinkle with cashew pieces.
- Return to oven and continue baking, uncovered, for another 10 minutes.
- Serve as a side with your traditional holiday meal.

172. Favorite Macaroni And Cheese Recipe

Serving: 20 | Prep: | Cook: 45mins | Ready in:

Ingredients

- 8-12 oz elbow macaroni
- one stick of butter
- 10 cups assorted cheeses
- 2 cups heavy whipping cream
- 2 cups milk
- 1/2 c flour
- salt to taste
- pepper to taste
- one sleeve of Ritz vegetable crackers

Direction

- Preheat oven to 375 degrees
- Spray a 9x13 baking pan/dish
- Boil elbow macaroni until soft. Pour in drainer and let sit.
- In same pot, melt one stick of butter.
- Add in flour whisking constantly
- Slowly add whipping cream and milk
- Let simmer/boil for about 8 minutes (mixture will become thick)
- Add in half of your grated cheese
- Add in your drained, cooked macaroni
- Pour mixture in baking pan/dish
- Top with remainder cheese
- Crush vegetable Ritz crackers very fine and sprinkle on top
- Cook about 30-45 minutes

173. Feta Cheese Filler For Baked Potato Recipe

Serving: 1 | Prep: | Cook: 10mins | Ready in:

Ingredients

- 200g feta cheese
- 3g of dried dill
- 1 tablespoon of butter

Direction

- Mix together until you get a homogenous mass

174. Fish Fillets Baked With Potatoes Recipe

Serving: 4 | Prep: | Cook: 30mins | Ready in:

Ingredients

- 800 gr white fresh fish fillets
- 4 green onions
- 4 rather large potatoes
- 2 tomatoes sliced into rings
- 6 tablespoons olive oil + extra for pan
- 2/3 cup white dry wine
- 2 bay leaves
- thyme, salt and pepper

Direction

- Peel the potatoes, put them in a pan cover with cold water and salt. Boil for 12-15 minutes and drain. Let them cool slightly and cut into thin slices. Clean the onions, cut in slices and cut the tender, green part in diagonal pieces.
- Preheat oven to 180 ° C. Put the fish fillets in the centre of an oiled fireproof dish and place all around the potatoes, alternating with the onions and tomatoes. Add the bay leaves, thyme, salt and pepper, sprinkle with wine and 3 tablespoons olive oil, cover the pan with aluminum foil and put it in the oven for about 20 minutes.
- Check if the potatoes are well softened, remove the foil and sprinkle with the remaining olive oil. Turn on the grill of your oven and out the pan back and leave for 5 more minutes, until the potatoes are golden brown. Serve the fillets directly from the pan.

175. Fondant Potatoes Recipe

Serving: 6 | Prep: | Cook: | Ready in:

Ingredients

- 3 large whole russet potatoes
- 2 tablespoons high-heat-resistant vegetable oil, such as grape seed oil, I used garlic infused avocado.
- salt and ground black pepper to taste
- 3 tablespoons butter, I used 2 tbs Earth Balance
- 4 sprigs thyme, I used a generous pinch of dried
- 1/2 cup chicken broth, or more as needed

Direction

- Preheat oven to 425 degrees F (220 degrees C).
- Cut off ends of russet potatoes, stand potatoes on end, and peel potatoes from top to bottom with a sharp knife to make each potato into a uniform cylinder. Cut each cylinder in half crosswise to make 6 potato cylinders about 2 inches long.
- Place potatoes into a bowl of cold water for about 5 minutes to remove starch from outsides; pat dry with paper towels.
- Place a heavy oven-proof skillet (such as a cast iron skillet) over high heat. Pour in vegetable oil; heat oil until it shimmers slightly.
- Place potato cylinders with best-looking ends into the hot oil, lower heat to medium-high, and pan-fry potatoes until well-browned, 5 to

6 minutes. The first side took 6 minutes and the second took 4.
- Season with salt and black pepper.
- Flip the potatoes onto the opposite ends. After they cook, use a paper towel held with tongs to carefully blot out the oil from the skillet. Add butter and thyme sprigs to skillet.
- Pick up a thyme sprig with tongs and use it to paint butter over the top of the potatoes. Since I used dried I spooned the liquid over the potatoes. Cook until butter foams and foam turns from white to a pale tan colour. Season with more salt and pepper. Pour chicken stock into skillet.
- Transfer skillet to preheated oven and cook until potatoes are tender and creamy inside, about 30 minutes. If potatoes aren't tender, add 1/4 cup more stock and let cook 10 more minutes. Mine to a total of 45 mins and I had to add 1/4 cup more stock twice.
- Place potatoes on a serving platter and spoon thyme-scented butter remaining in skillet over potatoes. Garnish with thyme sprigs. Let cool about 5 minutes before serving.

176. Fragrant Chicken And Potato Bake Recipe

Serving: 4 | Prep: | Cook: 40mins | Ready in:

Ingredients

- 4 medium to large size potatoes, with skin
- 1/2 rotisserie chicken, or 1 lbs of raw ground chicken meat
- 4 shallots
- 2 tbsp butter
- 2 eggs
- 1 cup heavy cream
- 1 tsp salt
- 1/2 tsp ground black pepper
- 1/4 tsp each: sage, crushed rosemary or italian seasoning (optional)

Direction

- Grate potatoes using a coarse grater
- If you are using rotisserie chicken, separate meat from the bones and mince the meat in the processor
- Heat butter in a skillet over medium heat
- Mince or finely chop shallots and sauté in butter until nicely browned
- In a large mixing bowl, combine potatoes, chicken meat, eggs, cooked shallots, salt, pepper, herbs, and cream
- Mix well
- Fold out the mix into a square 8" casserole dish
- Heat the oven at 375&degress F
- Place the casserole dish in the middle of the oven and cook for about 40 minutes, or until top of the dish is nicely golden-browned
- Let stand for a few minutes after baking
- Serve hot

177. French Onion Potato Bake Recipe

Serving: 8 | Prep: | Cook: 27mins | Ready in:

Ingredients

- 6 large potaoes
- 250ml cream
- 1 large onion
- 2 pkts of French onion soup
- 2 cups of tasty cheese
- salt and pepper to season

Direction

- Heat the oven on 180c. Peel potatoes and slice them as thin as possible about a one eight of an inch. I use a slicer that make the job a lot easier and quicker. Put these aside. Peel the onion and slice exactly like the potatoes. Get a Foil tray (as I hate washing up) but you can make this in a casserole dish about four to five inches deep. Spray the bottom with some

Olive Oil spray, pour about 50mls of the cream on the bottom. Now start layering the casserole dish with potatoes first, then a layer of onions and generously sprinkle some French onion soup. Start again with the cream and potatoes, onions and the soup mix. You should be able to have about three layers. Finish on top with a fair bit of cheese (and sometimes I cover the chees with a layer of breadcrumbs mixed with some garlic) this gives the dish a totally different taste and a nice crusty top. Put in the oven and bake at 200c for about 20 to 30 minutes or until the potatoes are cooked. Enjoy

178. Fresh Filler For Baked Potato Recipe

Serving: 0 | Prep: | Cook: 10mins | Ready in:

Ingredients

- onions
- egg
- Fresh dill

Direction

- Chop a hardboiled egg and some onion add dill and simply mix in to the potato mass

179. Fried Japaleno Sliced Peppers Recipe

Serving: 0 | Prep: | Cook: 20mins | Ready in:

Ingredients

- 1 1/2 to 2 cups of sliced jalpaleno pepper
- about 1 teaspoon of mustard
- 1 cup of flour or your favorite to dust the japalenos in
- ! zip lock bag
- One deep fryer or a skillett ... with enough Oil to fry
- Plate and paper towel on the plate
- Tongs or some kind of cooking Utensil to use to take out the japalenos out of hot oil.

Direction

- Take peppers out of the jar without the juice then put the teaspoon of mustard on top and mix then in the zip lock bag put the flour
- Then add the jalapenos into it and Shake.
- Once your Oil is hot in your fryer... drop each jalapeno into the oil. A few at a time to fry... let fry until light brown... after they are light brown take them out using your Tongs or cooking Utensil...an place on plate that has your paper towel on

180. GUADALAJARA BAKED POTATOES Recipe

Serving: 4 | Prep: | Cook: 60mins | Ready in:

Ingredients

- 4 large baking potatoes
- 1 lb ground beef
- 1 med onion chopped
- 1 16oz can baked beans
- 1 can mild chopped green chilies
- 3/4 cup salsa
- 1 tsp cumin
- Grated Monterey Jack or pepperjack cheese

Direction

- Preheat oven to 450F.
- Place potatoes on a cookie sheet and bake for 30 minutes. Puncture with a fork and bake until tender, about 30 more minutes. Brown beef in a large skillet over med-high heat, stirring occasionally to break up clumps.
- Drain fat.

- Add onions and cook until soft, about 10-12 minutes.
- Add beans, chilies, salsa and cumin; heat through.
- Split potato in half and pour meat mixture over them.
- Top with grated cheese

181. Garden Stuffed Baked Potatoes Recipe

Serving: 4 | Prep: | Cook: 45mins | Ready in:

Ingredients

- 4 russet potatoes
- 2 tablespoons butter or margarine
- 1 small onion chopped
- 1 (10 ounce) package frozen chopped broccoli, thawed, drained
- 1/2 cup ranch salad dressing
- 1 tablespoon vegetable oil
- 2 teaspoons dried parsley; optional
- salt
- pepper

Direction

- Preheat oven to 425 F.
- Pierce potatoes and microwave on HIGH for 12 minutes; or bake for 15 minutes.
- Slice off potato tops.
- Scoop out pulp, keeping skin intact.
- Mash pulp in a medium sized bowl.
- Heat a small skillet over medium heat; add butter.
- Add onion and sauté' until tender, about 5 minutes.
- Add onion, broccoli, and salad dressing, to potato pulp; mix well.
- Brush outside of potato skins shells with oil.
- Spoon potato mixture into skins, dividing evenly.
- Place potatoes on a baking sheet.
- Bake potatoes until heated through, about 15 minutes.
- Sprinkle with parsley; salt and pepper to taste.

182. Garlic Baked Potatoes Recipe

Serving: 6 | Prep: | Cook: 60mins | Ready in:

Ingredients

- 6 large potatoes scrubbed
- 3 teaspoons olive oil
- 1 tablespoon fresh rosemary finely chopped
- 1 tablespoon freshly ground black pepper
- 6 cloves garlic peeled and cut

Direction

- Preheat barbecue to medium heat.
- Using an apple corer carefully remove plug from each potato making sure not to go through potato.
- Reserve the plugs.
- Combine oil, rosemary and black pepper.
- Fill hole in each potato with two garlic halves and a little oil mixture.
- Cut off two thirds of each plug and discard.
- Replace remaining plug in potato and wrap potatoes in aluminum foil.
- Cook on barbecue for 1 hour.

183. Gotta Be Ultimate Double Baked Potato Boats Recipe

Serving: 6 | Prep: | Cook: 120mins | Ready in:

Ingredients

- 3 large baking potatoes
- 8 ounces cheddar cheese, shredded

- French onion dip (8 ounces)
- 1 stick unsalted butter, room temperature
- 3 green onions, thinly sliced, including the green part
- 3 dashes louisiana hot sauce
- salt and pepper to taste

Direction

- Wash and scrub potatoes
- Wrap in foil
- Bake for 2 hours at 350 degrees
- When baked, remove from oven, cool, slice in half
- Using a teaspoon, scoop the potatoes, leaving only a potato "boat"
- In a medium bowl, mash the scooped potatoes thoroughly
- Add the softened butter, French Onion Dip, cheese, sliced green onions, hot sauce, salt, and pepper to taste
- Mix well
- Mound the mixture back into the empty potato "boats"
- Place in a baking pan or on a cookie sheet
- Bake again at 350 degrees for about 30 more minutes

184. Greek Potato Bake Recipe

Serving: 6 | Prep: | Cook: 30mins | Ready in:

Ingredients

- 6 medium potatoes peeled and quartered
- 1 small bunch fresh thyme
- 2 garlic cloves crushed
- 4 small ripe tomatoes
- 1/2 teaspoon salt
- 1 teaspoon freshly ground black pepper
- 1/4 cup olive oil
- 1/4 cup white wine

Direction

- Preheat oven to 350 then place potatoes, thyme, garlic and tomatoes in a roasting pan.
- Season with salt and pepper the mix olive oil and wine and pour over potatoes.
- Cover roasting pan with aluminum foil and seal the edges.
- Bake 30 minutes then serve while warm.

185. Grilled Baked Potatoes Recipe

Serving: 4 | Prep: | Cook: 25mins | Ready in:

Ingredients

- 4 medium baking potatoes, scrubbed
- 1 Tbsp. oil
- 1 tsp. salt
- 1/2 cup sour cream
- 1/2 cup Shredded cheddar cheese
- 1/4 cup sliced green onions
- 1/4 cup Real bacon bits

Direction

- PREHEAT grill to medium-high heat. Pierce potatoes with fork or small sharp knife. Rub with oil; sprinkle with salt.
- PLACE potatoes on microwaveable plate. Microwave on HIGH 8 min. or until tender, turning after 4 min. Place potatoes on greased grate of grill.
- COOK 12 to 15 min. or until potatoes are crisp and browned, turning occasionally. Split potatoes. Serve topped with remaining ingredients.
- KRAFT KITCHENS TIPS: Note
- Microwaved potatoes can also be wrapped individually in foil. Grill 12 to 15 min. or until potatoes are tender, turning occasionally. Potatoes will be less crispy than when grilled without the foil.
- Substitute:

- Prepare as directed, using Reduced Fat or Light Sour Cream and KRAFT 2% Milk Shredded Reduced Fat Cheddar Cheese.
- Recipe courtesy of Kraft Kitchens

186. Ham And Cheese Potato Bake Recipe

Serving: 12 | Prep: | Cook: 75mins | Ready in:

Ingredients

- 1 24-oz. package of frozen hash browns, not tater tots
- 2 cups cubed fully cooked ham
- 3/4 cup shredded cheddar cheese, divided
- 1 small onion, chopped
- 2 cups sour cream
- 1 10 3/4 oz. can condensed cheddar cheese soup, undiluted
- 1 10 3/4 oz. can condensed cream of potato soup, unidluted
- (I usually just use 2 cans mushroom soup because I always have it!)
- 1/4 tsp. pepper

Direction

- In a large bowl, combine potatoes, ham, 1/2 cup cheese and onion. In another bowl, combine sour cream, soups and pepper; add to potato mixture and mix well.
- Transfer to a greased 3 quart baking dish. Sprinkle with remaining cheese. Bake, uncovered, at 350 F for 60 to 65 minutes or until bubbly and potatoes are tender. Let stand for 10 minutes before serving.

187. Hasselback Potatoes With Seasoned Breadcrumbs Recipe

Serving: 8 | Prep: | Cook: 2hours | Ready in:

Ingredients

- 8 medium russet potatoes (6 to 8 ounces each)
- 5 tablespoons butter, melted
- 1 teaspoon salt
- 3 tablespoons seasoned fine dry bread crumbs
- 2 tablespoons grated Parmesan cheese
- 1 tablespoon snipped fresh chives
- 1 teaspoon snipped fresh thyme

Direction

- Preheat oven to 375 degrees F. Fill a large bowl with water. Place potatoes in water bowl. Gather two 1/2-inch-thick chopsticks or two 1/2-inch-thick wooden spoons; set aside.
- For potatoes, slice a thin slice, lengthwise from the bottom of each potato, so they can stand without rolling on the cutting board. Arrange chopsticks or wooden spoons lengthwise on opposite sides of one potato on the cutting board. Slice potato crosswise into 1/8-inch-thick slices, stopping the knife when it reaches the chopsticks or the wooden spoons to prevent slicing all the way through. Return sliced potato to water bowl. Repeat with remaining potatoes.
- Line a 15x10x1-inch baking pan with foil; grease foil. Drain potatoes well and pat dry. Arrange potatoes in the prepared baking pan. Brush evenly with 2 tablespoons of the melted butter and sprinkle with 1/2 teaspoon of the salt. Cover with foil. Bake for 45 minutes. Uncover. Bake for 10 to 15 minutes more or until tender. Remove from oven. Turn oven to broil.
- Preheat broiler. In a small bowl stir together bread crumbs, cheese, chives, thyme, and the remaining 1/2 teaspoon salt. Sprinkle potatoes evenly with crumb mixture. Slowly and carefully spoon on remaining 3 tablespoons

- melted butter, being sure to cover all of the crumb mixture.
- Broil potatoes 4 to 5 inches from the heat for 2 to 3 minutes or until topping is golden. Serve immediately.
- From the Test Kitchen
- To Make Ahead:
- Prepare potatoes as directed through Step 2. Cover bowl and store in the refrigerator for up to 24 hours. Drain potatoes well.
- Nutrition Facts (Hassel back Potatoes with Seasoned Breadcrumbs)
- Per serving: 178 kcal cal., 8 g fat (5 g sat. fat, 0 g polyunsaturated fat, 2 g monounsaturated fat), 20 mg cholesterol, 418 mg sodium, 24 g carb., 3 g fibre, 1 g sugar, 4 g pro. Percent Daily Values are based on a 2,000 calorie diet

188. Herb And Onion Baked Potatoes Recipe

Serving: 4 | Prep: | Cook: 60mins | Ready in:

Ingredients

- 4 baking potatoes (about oz each)
- 4 tsp olive oil
- 1 tsp dried basil
- 1 tsp sea salt or kosher salt
- 1/2 tsp dried oregano
- 1/4 tsp black pepper (approximately)
- 1/2 c. onion, finely chopped
- 1 Tbsp minced garlic

Direction

- Preheat oven to 475
- Cut 1 potato lengthwise into quarters; place on a 12 inch square of foil.
- Brush cut sides of potato with 1 tsp. oil, sprinkle with 1/4 tsp. each basil and salt, 1/8 tsp. oregano, and a dash of pepper. Top with 2 Tbsp. onion and 3/4 tsp. garlic.
- Reassemble potato and wrap tightly in foil.
- Repeat for remaining potatoes.
- Place wrapped potatoes on bottom rack in oven, bake for 1 hour or until tender.

189. Home Style Turkey And Potato Bake Recipe

Serving: 4 | Prep: | Cook: 70mins | Ready in:

Ingredients

- 1 pouch Betty Crocker® roasted garlic mashed potatoes (from 7.2-oz box)
- 1 cup hot water
- 1/2 cup milk
- 2 tablespoons butter or margarine
- 2 cups chopped cooked turkey
- 1 bag (12 oz) Green Giant® Valley Fresh Steamers™ frozen mixed vegetables, thawed
- 1 jar (12 oz) home-style turkey gravy
- 1/4 teaspoon poultry seasoning

Direction

- Heat oven to 350°F. Spray 2-quart casserole with cooking spray; set aside. Make mashed potatoes as directed on box for 4 servings — (or use leftover mashers from dinner) except use 1 cup hot water, 1/2 cup milk and 2 tablespoons butter.
- In 2-quart saucepan, heat turkey, vegetables, gravy and poultry seasoning to boiling over medium-high heat, stirring occasionally. Pour turkey mixture into casserole. Spoon or pipe potatoes around edge of casserole.
- Bake uncovered 35 to 40 minutes or until mixture bubbles around edge of casserole.
- You can also pipe the potatoes on to make it prettier.

190. Honey Butter Baked Chicken With Mashed Sweet Potatoes Recipe

Serving: 4 | Prep: | Cook: 60mins | Ready in:

Ingredients

- 1 (3 to 3 1/2-pound) whole chicken, rinsed and patted dry
- 1 tablespoon kosher salt
- 1/2 teaspoon fresh cracked black pepper
- 6 tablespoons honey
- 1 lemon, zested
- 1 tablespoon lemon juice
- 1 tablespoon room temperature unsalted butter
- 1 tablespoon fresh thyme leaves
- mashed sweet potatoes, recipe follows
- Mashed Sweet Potatoes:
- 2 pounds sweet potatoes
- 1/2 cup heavy cream
- 3 tablespoons light brown sugar
- 3 tablespoons butter
- 2 tablespoons cane or maple syrup
- Pinch salt and pepper
- 1 teaspoon fresh thyme leaves, optional
- Preheat the oven to 350 degrees F.
- Place the potatoes on a foil lined baking sheet and bake until tender and begins to ooze sugary syrup, about 1 hour and 15 minutes. Remove from the oven and let sit until cool enough to handle.
- Cut the potatoes in half lengthwise and scoop out the flesh with a spoon into a large bowl. Add the cream, sugar, butter, syrup, salt and pepper, and thyme, if using and mix, mashing until the potato mixture is smooth. Cover to keep warm until ready to serve.

Direction

- Preheat the oven to 400 degrees F. Arrange a rack inside a large roasting pan and set aside.
- Season the chicken both inside and out with the kosher salt and black pepper.
- In a small bowl, combine the honey, lemon zest and juice and butter. Place the chicken on a rack in a roasting pan breast side up and roast until lightly browned, about 15 minutes. Using a pastry brush, brush half of the honey mixture over the chicken, as well as sprinkling half the thyme over the chicken and return the chicken to the oven. Continue to cook another 30 minutes, or until an instant-read thermometer inserted in the thickest part of the thigh registers 180 degrees F. Remove the chicken from the oven and brush the remaining honey blend and sprinkle the remainder of the thyme over the chicken.
- Remove the chicken from the oven and transfer to a platter or cutting board to rest for 10 minutes before carving.
- To serve, spoon the sweet potatoes into the centre of 4 large plates and arrange the chicken on top. Drizzle the chicken with any remaining pan juices and serve immediately with the sweet potatoes.

191. In A Hurry But Yummy Potato Bake Recipe

Serving: 46 | Prep: | Cook: 45mins | Ready in:

Ingredients

- 3 potatoes, large
- 2 sweet potatoes med. size
- 1/2 butternut pumpkin
- 3 garlic corms(whol garlic)
- 600ml cream
- salt; pepper to taste
- 2cups tasty cheese, grated

Direction

- Pre-heat oven to 180deg C
- Peel and cut vegetables to bite size pieces
- Steam in microwave till soft, time will depend on the oven, 4-5 min.

- While veg is steaming, put whole garlic in small pan, with a little olive oil, cook slowly until soft, with lid on. You will know when cooked by the smell, sugary. Approx. 10 to 15min
- Squeeze the garlic to extract the pulp. If you don't want to go to all this trouble, you can just use crushed garlic, about 3 fat cloves
- In an oven proof dish place the drained veg, the garlic, cream, (you may not use all the cream, but you need enough to cover toe veg), a little fresh ground pepper, salt if you like, top with cheese.
- Place in a preheated oven 180deg C for approx. 25-30min, or until the cheese is golden...
- Great to bring a plate to a party, barbecue, or picnic, as it transports easily.
- Enjoy.

192. Italian Potato Topped Chicken Bake Recipe

Serving: 4 | Prep: | Cook: 30mins | Ready in:

Ingredients

- 1 cup cooked chicken
- 1 can peas (or any vegetable you like)
- 1 can cream of chicken soup
- 1/2 cup milk
- a heaping cup of instant potatoes
- 1 egg
- 2/3 cup water
- 1/3 cup Italian salad dressing
- cheese

Direction

- Preheat oven to 350
- In a saucepan-mix chicken, drained peas, soup. Heat to bubbly. Pour into an 8 x 8 pan.
- In saucepan (I use the same one) heat water, milk and dressing. Add the potato flakes. Let stand 1 minutes. Add egg and blend well.

- Cool a couple of minutes.
- Place potatoes in a zip lock bag. Cut off the tip and pipe potatoes around the edge of the casserole.
- Sprinkle with cheese.
- Bake 350 degrees for 30 minutes or until potatoes are set and light golden brown.

193. Killer Baked Sweet Potatoes Recipe

Serving: 46 | Prep: | Cook: 45mins | Ready in:

Ingredients

- 4 sweet potatoes, scrubbed
- honey or brown sugar
- butter
- 1 Tsp vanilla
- A little milk (just a smidgeon)
- 1 cup Chopped pecans (I love my food processor for this)
- marshmallows (optional. Baby marshmallows handle better, but the big marshmallow covers more area.)

Direction

- Cook the sweet potatoes until soft and squishy. (You can microwave if in a hurry or they are taking longer than your other dishes)
- Remove from heat and split in half.
- Carefully scoop out the middle meat, leaving the skin intact (like a boat)
- Take the sweet potato meat and mix in the honey (or brown sugar), butter, milk, and vanilla.
- Beat until fluffy.
- Scoop mix back into skins and top with marshmallows (if using press them firmly down into the potato mix) and chopped pecans.
- Cook for an additional 15 minutes or until the marshmallow has melted, oozed down into the potato, and covers the top of the potato.

- Remove from heat, place on plate, and serve.
- NOTE: Taste the filling as you mix it to see if you want to increase either the seasonings or the sweetness. I have used pumpkin pie spice in this as well as maple syrup with good results.
- Enjoy!

194. Killer Italian Baked Potatoes Recipe

Serving: 6 | Prep: | Cook: 52mins | Ready in:

Ingredients

- About 6-8 peeled potoatoes
- 1 bottle on Good Seasons Italian dressing made at home from package mix.
- Extra couple of cloves of fresh squeezed garlic for those who love garlic.

Direction

- Wash and peel potatoes.
- Cut in half lengthwise.
- Lay flat cut side down. It is now easy to slice the potato!
- Slice thin as possible (like making potatoes chips). Why thin? Dressing penetrates better.
- In a large mixing bowl, add potatoes and a lot of the dressing (oil, vinegar, water and packet of mix) that has been made ahead of time. I have a plastic container that I make use to make two packages of the Italian Seasoning. It doesn't last long in this house. This is good for adding to 3-4 bean salad to kick it up a notch.
- Using a large mixing bowl, stir the potatoes and dressing until all sides of every slice is coated. Mix it up good. This is when you can add extra fresh squeezed garlic.
- Pour into a 9 x 12 glass baking dish, pour on some more dressing over the dish of potatoes.
- Bake at 375 for at least 45 minutes (longer if necessary) until the top is looking crispy. When the top is crisp so is the bottom layer

against the glass. These are the layers we fight over. I salt and pepper after dishing to the plate. Yummy smell when cooking and "oh" the taste buds when eaten! Enjoy. JJ

195. Leahs Baked Scalloped Potatoes Au Gratin Recipe

Serving: 6 | Prep: | Cook: 120mins | Ready in:

Ingredients

- 6 medium sized potatoes - sliced thin as possible. To cheat, use your food processor slicing blade, and put slices in cold water until all are finished sliced. And figure 1.5 potatoes per hungry person.
- 2 cups milk - whole milk is better, you can use chicken or vegetable broth for those who are lactose intolerant or vegan...or for those who simply forgot to buy milk that day
- 1 medium onion diced
- 1/2 stick butter cut up into little bits (I didn't say this recipe is dietetic, so ok - don't blame the cook - lol
- 5 tablespoons flour
- 1 and 1/2 teaspoon salt
- 1 teaspoon fresh cracked pepper
- 2 tablespoons fresh rosemary (optional but oh so good)
- 1 cup shredded cheese - but use a combination of three cheeses if you can such as Parmesan, Cheddar, and Gouda. Great to use any leftover cheeses you need to "get rid of".
- Equipment needed: Casserole Dish or oven-ready deep skillet for a crispier dish. Lid or tinfoil to cover dish while baking until last 30 minutes of baking time.

Direction

- Preheat oven at 350 degrees, or put it in at whatever your oven temp is at while you are roasting your meat or poultry. This dish is very flexible, but adjust time according to your oven temp, at lower temperature it will obviously need a little more time. And it is like making lasagne, you will simply be making layers with the ingredients.

- O.k. starting with that casserole dish, butter it up but good including the sides.
- Next starting with those sliced potatoes, place in a circle creating a layer of potatoes. Make sure you leave the nice perfect slices for the top layer.
- Combine all other ingredients in separate bowl except for liquid to make layering process easier. Mix till flour and cheese are well incorporated.
- Sprinkle this mixture over your first layer of potatoes.
- Guess what? Start all over with a new layer of potatoes and repeat process of sprinkling remaining ingredients except for milk.
- Once you have completed all your layering, you now know how to layer bricks for your next home improvement project - ok just kidding here folks, just making sure you are paying attention. Back to business...
- Next add enough of your chosen liquid to just cover the potatoes.
- Cover with lid or tin foil and shove the darn dish into that oven of yours. You can prepare this dish up to 3 hours ahead and leave it in fridge till ready to bake.
- At last half hour, remove lid/tinfoil. If potatoes are not looking brown enough for you, you can certainly turn up the oven, but pay attention to avoid burning cheese topping. Let stand a bit before serving - perfect while the roast is resting as well.
- And call your peeps to the dinner table to enjoy!

196. Lemon Baked Potatoes Recipe

Serving: 4 | Prep: | Cook: 60mins | Ready in:

Ingredients

- 4 large russet potatoes
- 1/2 cup lemon juice
- 1/2 teaspoon salt
- 1/2 teaspoon freshly ground black pepper
- 4 cloves garlic minced
- 1 tablespoon dried oregano
- 1 cup extra virgin olive oil
- 1/2 teaspoon paprika

Direction

- Peel and wash potatoes then cut them lengthwise into quarters and place in a bowl.
- Pour lemon juice over them and toss then add salt, pepper, minced garlic, oregano and oil.
- Mix well and marinate at least 1 hour then preheat oven to 425.
- Arrange potatoes in one layer in baking pan.
- Pour marinade over top and sprinkle with paprika.
- Cover pan and put on lower rack of oven then bake 25 minutes.
- Uncover and bake 30 minutes or until potatoes are tender and crispy on top then serve hot.

197. Lemon Lime Baked Sweet Potatoes Recipe

Serving: 6 | Prep: | Cook: 40mins | Ready in:

Ingredients

- 1 cup brown sugar
- 7 ounces lemon lime soda
- 1/2 teaspoon salt
- 2 tablespoons margarine
- 1 teaspoon nutmeg
- 4 large sweet potatoes sliced

Direction

- In heavy skillet combine all ingredients except sweet potatoes.

- Boil together 5 minutes then add sweet potatoes and simmer 20 minutes.
- Place in 350 oven and bake 20 additional minutes.

198. Loaded Baked Potato Pizza Recipe

Serving: 8 | Prep: | Cook: 14mins | Ready in:

Ingredients

- 1 Homemade pizza crust
- 6   Slices (1 oz each) provolone cheese
- 2 C. Cubed unpeeled baked potato (about 1 large)
- 2 T.. olive oil
- 2 T. ranch dressing and seasoning mix (from 1-oz milk recipe package)
- 8   Strips crisply cooked bacon, chopped
- 1 C. Shredded mild cheddar cheese (4 oz)
- 1/4 C. Sliced green onions (4 medium), if desired
- sour cream, if desired

Direction

- Heat oven to 400°F.
- Grease 1 Large pizza pan.
- Throw some (about 1-2 tsp. or more) Corn meal on the pan.
- Place dough on pizza pan; starting at center, press dough into round shape.
- Arrange provolone cheese slices on dough.
- In medium bowl, mix potato, olive oil and ranch dressing mix. Spoon evenly over cheese.
- Sprinkle with bacon and Cheddar cheese.
- Bake 13 to 16 minutes or until crust is golden brown and cheese is melted.
- Sprinkle with onions.
- Serve with sour cream or whatever else you like on "loaded Baked Potatoes"

199. Loaded Baked Potato Recipe

Serving: 8 | Prep: | Cook: 110mins | Ready in:

Ingredients

- 4 baking potatoes (2 ½ lbs)
- 16 ounces ricotta cheese
- 1 to 2 tablespoons chopped chives
- 3 garlic cloves, roasted
- 1 ½ cups shredded Cheddar
- paprika

Direction

- Pierce the potatoes with a fork, and bake at 350-degrees for one hour and 20 minutes.
- Cut each potato in half, lengthwise and scoop out the pulp.
- Mash the pulp in a bowl with the Ricotta, chives, garlic and 1 cup of the Cheddar.
- Spoon this mixture back into the potato shells, piling it up nicely.
- Place the filled shells on a LIGHTLY greased baking sheet, and bake at 350-degrees for 15 to 20 minutes.
- Sprinkle with the remaining Cheddar, and bake 10 minutes more.
- Sprinkle with paprika to taste and for colour.

200. Loaded Baked Potato Salad Recipe

Serving: 8 | Prep: | Cook: 1mins | Ready in:

Ingredients

- 6-8 baking potatoes baked till done and then chilled
- 3/4 cup of mayo
- 1/4 cup of sour cream
- 1/2 tsp salt
- 1/4 tsp black pepper
- 1 bunch of sliced green onion

- 1 cup of bacon crumbles
- 1/2 cup of shredded cheddar cheese

Direction

- Bake potatoes, with olive oil and kosher salt. Cool, remove skins and dice or crumble potatoes.
- Toss remaining ingredients with potatoes mix well can add more mayo or sour cream if needed.
- Can also add green pepper, pimentos, white onion if desired.

201. Loaded Baked Potatoes Recipe

Serving: 4 | Prep: | Cook: 18mins | Ready in:

Ingredients

- 4 large baking potatoes
- 2 tablespoons butter, melted
- 3 tablespoons grated parmesan cheese
- 1/2 dried rosemary, crushed
- 1/4 teaspoon salt
- 1/8 teaspoon pepper
- 1/2 cup cheddar cheese, shredded
- 1/4 cup real bacon bits
- 1 green onion, chopped

Direction

- Scrub potatoes. With a sharp knife, sliced potatoes thinly but not all the way through, leaving slices attached at the bottom. Place on a microwave-safe plate; drizzle with butter.
- Combine the parmesan cheese, rosemary, salt and pepper; sprinkle over potatoes and between slices.
- Microwave, uncovered, and on high for 2-18 minutes or until potatoes are tender. Top with cheddar cheese, bacon and onion. Microwave for 1-2 minutes longer or until cheese is melted.

202. Loaded Mashed Potato Bake Recipe

Serving: 5 | Prep: | Cook: 10mins | Ready in:

Ingredients

- 1 container refrigerated mashed potatoes
- 1 pkg herbed cheese spread (alloutte is what i use)
- 1/4 C milk
- 1 pkg bacon pieces
- 1 1/2 C shredded cheddar cheese (divided)
- chives to garnish

Direction

- Prepare Potatoes as directed on package.
- In a large bowl combine warmed potatoes, cheese spread, bacon pieces, milk and 1 C of cheese together.
- Transfer mixture to a 9X9 inch baking dish and top with remaining cheese.
- Bake at 350 for 10-15min.
- Garnish with chives before serving.

203. Low Carb Baked Potatoes Recipe

Serving: 3 | Prep: | Cook: 35mins | Ready in:

Ingredients

- 2 1/2 c of cooked cauliflower
- 1 dash of pepper
- 3/4 c of shredded cheddar cheese
- 3-6 slices cooked crumpled bacon
- 3 finely chopped green onions
- 1 dash of salt
- 1 c of sour cream

Direction

- Set your bacon and 1/4 c of cheese aside because you are going to be using that last.
- Cut your cauliflower into little pieces
- In a medium mixing bowl start adding everything
- Preheat your oven to 350 F
- Place everything into your baking dish
- When that's done then sprinkle your bacon and the rest of your cheese on top. Bake for 20 minutes

204. MASHED NEW POTATO CHEESE BAKE WITH GARLIC Recipe

Serving: 4 | Prep: | Cook: 50mins | Ready in:

Ingredients

- MASHED new potato CHEESE BAKE WITH garlic
- 3/4 c. seasoned dry bread crumbs
- 3 c. mashed New (red) potatoes
- 2 CHOPPED cloves garlic (ccok with potatoes)
- 2 eggs
- 1/2 c. parmesan cheese
- 8 oz. sliced mozzarella cheese
- 2 tbsp. butter, softened
- 1/4 teaspoon paprika
- pinch ground red pepper
- (Garnish optional: small amount chopped fresh dill)

Direction

- Sprinkle 1/4 cup bread crumbs in greased baking dish.
- Set aside.
- Mix mashed potatoes, eggs seasonings and Parmesan together.
- Spread half of mixture in baking dish and top with Mozzarella.
- Spread remaining potatoes over cheese.
- Mix remaining bread crumbs and butter together and sprinkle on top.
- Bake 50-60 minutes at 350 degrees.
- Let stand 15 minutes before serving.

205. Marinated Potatoes Recipe

Serving: 8 | Prep: | Cook: | Ready in:

Ingredients

- 8 medium potatoes
- 5 bay leaves
- 5 cloves garlic
- 1 lemon
- 1 cinnamon stick
- 1 tablespoon honey
- 1 tablespoon brown sugar
- 1 teaspoon rosemary
- 1 teaspoon cumin
- 1 tablespoon mustard
- 1 tablespoon pepper mix
- 5 tablespoons balsamic vinegar
- 5 tablespoons olive oil
- 5 tablespoons soy sauce

Direction

- Wash potatoes well as the use in shell, cut in half and set aside. In a mortar, put the laurel, garlic, cinnamon, rosemary, cumin, peppercorns and crush them. Place in a mixing bowl with the sliced lemon, honey, mustard, vinegar, olive oil and soy sauce and mix to incorporate all the potatoes. Place in a dish with a lid, and sprinkle with brown sugar, bring them to a moderate oven until potatoes are golden. You can also cook on the stovetop in a pan or similar.

206. Mashed Potato And Gravy Bake Recipe

Serving: 8 | Prep: | Cook: 35mins | Ready in:

Ingredients

- Leftover mashed potatoes (I use butter, milk, sour cream and cream cheese)
- Leftover gravy
- Grated cheese

Direction

- Use your favourite casserole or baking dish.
- Layer 1-1/2 of the leftover potatoes on bottom.
- Layer 2-all gravy.
- Layer 3-Grated cheese.
- Layer 4-Remaining mashed potatoes.
- Layer 5-Grated Cheese.
- Cover. Put in 350 oven for 35 minutes. Remove cover and bake an additional 10.
- Variations: add a layer of onions, bacon, green pepper.....
- Use the ingredients you like and make it your own!!!!

207. Mashed Potato Bake Recipe

Serving: 4 | Prep: | Cook: 15mins | Ready in:

Ingredients

- 3 large baking potatoes, peeled and cut into cubes
- 1 package (10 ounces) frozen chopped spinach, thawed
- 1/2 cup heavy cream
- 3 tablespoons butter
- 1/2 teaspoon salt
- 1/2 teaspoon pepper
- Topping
- 1/2 cup Italian-style bread crumbs
- 3 tablespoons grated parmesan cheese
- 3 tablespoons melted butter
- 1 teaspoon dried parsley

Direction

- Preheat oven to 375°F. Lightly grease a medium casserole dish.
- Place potatoes in a medium pot. Add enough water to cover; bring to a boil. Cook until tender, about 20 minutes. Drain and transfer to a medium bowl. Mash potatoes in bowl.
- Gradually add spinach, cream, butter, salt and pepper to bowl; mix until just combined. Transfer potato mixture to prepared dish; smooth top.
- For topping, in a small bowl, combine bread crumbs, Parmesan and melted butter. Sprinkle topping evenly over potato mixture. Bake until topping is golden, about 15 minutes. Sprinkle parsley over top. Serve immediately.
- Tips: Mashing Success
- For best results, cook potatoes just until fork tender and drain thoroughly. To mash, use a hand masher, a potato ricer, a food mill, or an electric mixer. Be sure not to overbeat potatoes because they will become thick and pasty.

208. Mashed Potato Layer Bake Recipe

Serving: 14 | Prep: | Cook: 25mins | Ready in:

Ingredients

- 4 large white potatoes, peeled, chopped and cooked
- 2 large sweet potatoes, peeled, chopped and cooked
- 1 tub (8 oz.) chive & Onion cream cheese spread, divided
- 1/2 cup sour cream, divided
- 1/4 tsp. each salt and black pepper
- 1/4 cup Shredded or 100% Grated parmesan cheese, divided
- 1/4 cup Shredded cheddar cheese, divided

Direction

- PREHEAT oven to 375°F. Place potatoes in separate bowls. Add half each of the cream cheese and sour cream to each bowl; season with salt and pepper. Mash with potato masher or fork until creamy.
- STIR half of the Parmesan cheese into white potatoes. Stir half of the Cheddar cheese into sweet potatoes. Alternately layer half each of the white potato and sweet potato mixture in 2-qt. clear glass casserole. Repeat layers.
- BAKE 15 min. Sprinkle with remaining cheeses; bake 5 more min. or until cheeses are melted.
- Make Ahead: (Optional)
- Assemble casserole as directed. Do not add the cheese topping. Cover and refrigerate casserole and cheese topping separately up to 3 days. When ready to serve, uncover and bake casserole as directed, increasing baking time as needed until casserole is heated through. Top with remaining cheeses and continue as directed.

209. Mashed Potatoes Baked With Cream Recipe

Serving: 4 | Prep: | Cook: 40mins | Ready in:

Ingredients

- 4 potatoes
- 1 cup shredded medium cheddar cheese. or sharp if you prefer
- 1 cup or more cream
- 1 tbs. minced onion

Direction

- Boil potatoes and mash them
- Mix in onions that have been sautéed in butter.
- Add salt -pepper to taste
- Put into a casserole dish.
- Spread cheese on top
- Pour cream over to barely cover potatoes
- Bake in a 350 oven until cheese is browned

210. Mexican Baked Potatoes Recipe

Serving: 2 | Prep: | Cook: 1hours15mins | Ready in:

Ingredients

- 4 lg. baking potatoes
- 1 lb. ground beef
- 1 med. onion, chopped
- 1 lb. canned chili beans
- 4 oz. canned mild green chilies
- 1/2 tsp. ground cumin
- 3/4 c. tomato salsa
- Grated cheddar cheese

Direction

- Bake potatoes for 50 mins or more or until done inside, meanwhile, brown beef in a large skillet and discard fat. Add onions and cook until soft. Add chili beans, green chilies, cumin and salsa. Heat through. Split baked potatoes. Pour beef mixture over tops of potatoes. Top with grated cheese. Also a chopped ripe avocado may be added.

211. Microwave Dill Baked Potatoe Salad Recipe

Serving: 10 | Prep: | Cook: 30mins | Ready in:

Ingredients

- A couple bunches of green onions.
- a can of chopped black olives
- 1 1/2 tsp.-dill weed and couple of dill pickles chopped sm.pieces.
- 1 doz.-eggs

- 8 t0 10 -potatoes
- can cut up one or two stocks of celery if desired . chop in sm pieces.
- 1 1/2 to 2 cups of -mayonaise and 2 tsp.- white vinegar. sprinle of paprika for the top.

Direction

- Prepare the vegetables by chopping in to sm., about a nickel size pieces. Make sure you chop the dill pickles finely.
- Chop 1doz. hard boiled eggs, reserve two eggs for putting on the top for a garnishment.
- Green onions can be cut to the size you like but the potatoes that have been baked with skins on in the microwave - should be cut to nickel size pieces. Place all the above ingredients in to a bowel.do not peel the potatoes as this adds taste to the salad.
- Drain black olives and put into bowel with other ingredients.
- Mix up mayonnaise and dill weed and white vinegar in a bowel add a little water or milk to thin- till it can be poured, but not super thin over the potato salad. Add to above ingredients and mix. Add to the top of the salad two sliced hard boiled eggs and sprinkle with paprika to add color to salad. Chill and serve with dinner or lunch.

212. Mini Baked Potatoes With Blue Cheese Recipe

Serving: 10 | Prep: | Cook: 50mins | Ready in:

Ingredients

- 20 new, salad, or other miniature potatoes
- 4 T veg. oil
- coarse salt
- 1/2 c sour cream
- 1/4 c crumbled blue cheese
- 2 T chopped fresh chives

Direction

- Preheat oven to 350
- Wash and dry potatoes
- Toss with oil in large bowl, until coated
- Lightly roll potatoes in coarse salt, and place on baking sheet
- Bake 45-50 minutes, until tender
- Combine sour cream and blue cheese in small bowl
- Cut a cross in the top of each potato, and press gently with fingertips to open
- Top with generous spoonful of cheese mixture
- Garnish with chives

213. Mint & Sumac Rustic Potatoes Recipe

Serving: 0 | Prep: | Cook: 1hours | Ready in:

Ingredients

- 20 Mini red potatoes
- olive oil
- kosher salt
- ground black pepper
- Ground mint 1 teaspoon
- Sumac 1 tablespoon

Direction

- Cut the potatoes in halves or fourths depending on the size.
- Line a baking sheet with foil and coat with a thin layer of olive oil.
- Pour some olive oil in a bowl or cup & coat each piece of potato liberally. Place the coated potatoes on the baking sheet. Sprinkle and coat with a liberal amount of kosher salt and lightly with pepper, mint and sumac.
- Bake at 400 degrees for 45 minutes or when potatoes are soft & browned. I like to brown them to the point that they stick to the foil and crisp slightly.
- Serve with Tzatziki Sauce

214. Moose And Potato Bake Recipe

Serving: 6 | Prep: | Cook: 1mins | Ready in:

Ingredients

- 1 Moose roast or Tenderloin, Sliced to about 1/2 in thick
- 1 Can cream of mushroom soup (roasted garlic is the best)
- milk, Fill soup can with milk (about 1 cup)
- salt and pepper to taste
- garlic if not using roasted garlic cream of mushroom soup
- 2 large potatoes sliced thin, or enough to line a casserol dish about half way.
- 1 onion Sliced Thin

Direction

- Slice and season Moose Roast and set aside.
- Slice and season Potatoes and set aside.
- Spray casserole dish with Pam and lay out potatoes.
- Cover potatoes layer with onion slices.
- Cover onion with Moose steaks.
- Mix together soup and milk in bowl until well blended. Pour over Moose and cover and bake at 350 for about 1 hour, or until potatoes are tender.

215. Mushroom Filler For Baked Potato Recipe

Serving: 1 | Prep: | Cook: 10mins | Ready in:

Ingredients

- Marinated mushrooms
- garlic
- pickles
- tablespoon butter

Direction

- The garlic is optional but it does blend well with the other ingredients, the pickles are best chopped in to small cubes (10*10mm), mix in a bowl in to a salad and ad on top of the potato

216. Mustard Aioli Baked Potatoes With Herbs Recipe

Serving: 0 | Prep: | Cook: 60mins | Ready in:

Ingredients

- mustard Aioli:
- 1/3 cup mayonnaise
- 1 tablespoon Dijon mustard
- 1 tablespoon whole grain mustard
- 1 teaspoon honey
- 2 cloves garlic, smashed to a paste
- kosher salt and freshly ground black pepper
- Potatoes:
- 1 1/2 pounds small red-skinned potatoes, scrubbed, then halved or quartered
- 2 tablespoons kosher salt, plus more for sprinkling
- 1 medium onion, halved, peeled and sliced vertically
- Garnish:
- 1 tablespoon finely chopped fresh flat-leaf parsley
- 2 teaspoons finely chopped fresh chives
- 2 teaspoons finely chopped fresh tarragon
- Freshly ground black pepper and crushed red pepper flakes

Direction

- For the mustard aioli: Whisk the mayonnaise, Dijon mustard, whole grain mustard, honey and garlic and sprinkle with salt and pepper Cover the bowl and refrigerate for at least 30 minutes and up to 1 day

- Preheat your oven to 425 degrees. Meanwhile, Cut the potatoes in half or quartered, and onion toss with the mustard aioli.
- Grab a rimmed aluminum sheet pan and add the potatoes and sliced onions. Spread them out evenly before popping them into the oven to roast for 45-60 minutes. Stir them once halfway through.
- Once crispy and golden, season with kosher salt, black pepper, crushed red pepper flakes and the chopped fresh parsley, tarragon, chives.
- Enjoy.

217. Never Eat Another Potato But This One! Recipe

Serving: 2 | Prep: | Cook: 1hours30mins | Ready in:

Ingredients

- Never Eat Another potato but This One!
- Thx to Food.com and Viclynn
- Prep Time: 15 mins
- Total Time: 1 hrs 15 mins
- Serves: 2-20, Yield: 2.0 potatoes
- Ingredients
- red potatoes
- bacon - 1 slice for each potatoes
- onions, sliced - 1 slice for each potato

Direction

- Directions
- You choose quantities -- rinse and scrub potatoes.
- Slice potatoes in half, long end.
- Place a slice of onion in the middle of potato.
- Holding the 2 potato pieces, and onion, in place, wrap a piece of bacon around the long end, crisscross, and then the short end. Secure with a toothpick.
- Grill in disposable aluminum pan, on indirect, for 1 hour, turning to ensure bacon crisps evenly. Remove toothpicks before serving.
- I usually serve with sour cream. Enjoy!

218. New Baked Potatoes Recipe

Serving: 4 | Prep: | Cook: 20mins | Ready in:

Ingredients

- 1/4 c butter
- 8 new potatoes, scrubbed and cut in halves or quarters
- sea salt and ground black pepper

Direction

- Preheat oven to 350 degrees. Place butter in ovenproof baking pan and place in oven till butter is melted (about 3 to 4 mins). Remove pan from oven, add potatoes and toss with melted butter.
- Return potatoes to oven and bake for 20 mins, stirring occasionally until potatoes are tender when pierced with a knife. Season to taste with salt and pepper.

219. Nothing To It Baked Potato Restaurant Style Recipe

Serving: 6 | Prep: | Cook: 70mins | Ready in:

Ingredients

- 6 large baking potatoes, well scrubbed and patted dry
- 1/4 cup quality olive oil
- 1/4 cup coarse kosher or sea salt

Direction

- Place salt in shallow dish, large enough for a single potato to fit

- Lightly brush (or, like me, just use the two best kitchen tools you have...your hands! ;) olive oil over outside of each potato
- Roll each potato in salt (no need to cover, but should be present on all sides of the tater :)
- Place in centre of oven, directly on oven rack
- Bake at 375 for 60-70 minutes until fork tender
- Let cool slightly before serving
- Carefully open each potato and serve with butter and sour cream with chives or green onions.
- **Also a great base for a "loaded" baked potato**
- If you usually poke your taters, feel free to poke... otherwise, a good scrubbing should remove a few bits of skin, accomplishing the same thing! :)

220. One Pan Chicken And Potato Bake Recipe

Serving: 4 | Prep: | Cook: 60mins | Ready in:

Ingredients

- 4 bone-in chicken pieces (1-1/2 lbs)
- 1-1/2 lbs potatoes (about 3), cut in thin wedges
- 1/4 c zesty Italian dressing
- 1/4 c grated parmesan cheese
- 1 tsp italian seasoning

Direction

- Heat oven to 400 degrees. Place chicken and potatoes in 13x9" baking dish. Top with dressing; sprinkle with cheese and seasoning. Cover.
- Bake 1 hour or till chicken is done (165), uncovering after 30 mins.

221. Oven Baked Potato Wedges Recipe

Serving: 426 | Prep: | Cook: 30mins | Ready in:

Ingredients

- Pam cooking spray
- 6 tbsp. butter
- 4 lg. potatoes
- onion powder
- Donnie's cajun seasoning Mix (or equivalent) (Recipe on my recipe page)

Direction

- Preheat oven to 425 degrees.
- Scrub the potatoes, cut them in half lengthwise, and then cut each half in thirds lengthwise.
- You'll have 6 long wedges from each potato.
- Spray large cookie sheet (with sides) with cooking spray then add butter.
- Place pan in oven to melt butter.
- Remove pan from oven after butter is melted.
- Add potatoes to melted butter on cookie sheet.
- Spray potatoes with Pam then sprinkle on the onion powder and seasoning mix.
- Place cookie sheet back into oven and bake for 30 minutes or until potatoes are tender and evenly browned.

222. Oven Baked Potatoes Recipe

Serving: 4 | Prep: | Cook: 37mins | Ready in:

Ingredients

- red potatoes
- extra virgin olive oil
- thyme or rosemary
- garlic salt
- cracked black pepper

Direction

- Preheat oven to 400
- Cut red potatoes into 1/4 wedges-peels left on
- Spread out on a baking sheet
- Drizzle with EVOO
- Season with seasonings
- "Stir" potatoes so all are covered with EVOO & seasoning
- Bake for 30-45 mins, stirring once

223. Over Stuffed Chili Baked Potatoes Recipe

Serving: 8 | Prep: | Cook: 25mins | Ready in:

Ingredients

- chili-STUFFED POTATO SKINS
- .
- 4 large baking potatoes
- 2 tablespoons olive oil
- 2 cloves garlic, minced
- 1 small yellow onion, diced
- 1 tablespoon minced jarred jalapeno peppers
- 1 pound lean ground beef
- 1 cup canned crushed tomatoes
- 14-ounce can refried beans
- salt and ground black pepper, to taste
- 1 1/2 cups shredded cheddar cheese
- 2/3 cup ricotta cheese
- 1/2 cup milk

Direction

- Preheat oven to 425 degrees.
- Wash and dry the potatoes, then pierce each several times with a fork. Microwave (I prefer to oven-bake) on high for about 10 to 12 minutes, or until cooked through. Timing will vary by microwave.
- Meanwhile, in a medium saucepan over medium-high, combine the olive oil, garlic, onion and jalapenos. Sauté until the onion just begins to get tender, about 5 minutes. Add the ground beef and sauté until browned, about another 5 minutes.
- Add the crushed tomatoes and refried beans, then mix well and reduce heat to low. Bring to a simmer, season with salt and pepper, then cover and reduce heat to just keep warm.
- Carefully cut the potatoes in half lengthwise, then use a spoon to scoop out the insides and place them in a large bowl. Leave about 1/4 to 1/2 inch of potato all around the skin. Arrange the potato skins on a baking sheet. Set aside.
- To the bowl of potatoes, add 1 cup of the cheddar cheese, the ricotta and milk. Mix well, then season with salt and pepper. Set aside.
- Fill the potato skins almost to overflowing with the meat and bean mixture. Carefully spoon a bit of the potato and cheese mixture over the meat. Sprinkle each with some of the remaining cheddar.
- Bake until the cheese melts and the mashed potato topping just begins to brown, about 12 to 15 minutes.

224. POTATO BAKE Recipe

Serving: 4 | Prep: | Cook: 15mins | Ready in:

Ingredients

- 1 onion
- LITTLE oil
- COLD boiled potatoes
- GRATED MATURE cheddar cheese
- black pepper
- mixed herbs
- 1 CUP milk
- mustard
- tomato, IF DESIRED

Direction

- PREHEAT OVEN 200 DEGREEES C
- PEEL AND SLICE ONION AND COOK LIGHTLY IN A LITTLE OIL TILL SOFT

- SLICE PRE COOKED POTATOES AND LAYER IN OVEN PROOF DISH WITH SOFTENED ONIONS. AND GRATED CHEESE
- SEASON WITH BLACK PEPPER AND MIXED HERBS
- MEASURE A FULL MUG OF MILK AND MIX IN 1 TEASPOON MUSTARD
- POUR OVER THE POTATO MIX AND BAKE IN OVEN AND BAKE FOR 14 TO 20 MINUTES UNTIL GOLDEN BROWN. TOP WITH MORE GRATED CHEESE AND TOMATO IF DESIRED.
- ENJOY

225. Potato Bake Recipe

Serving: 10 | Prep: | Cook: 55mins | Ready in:

Ingredients

- 2 lb. package of O'brian type frozen potatoes
- 1 1/2 cups grated cheddar cheese
- 1/2 margarine or butter
- 1 cup cream of chicken soup
- 1 cup sour cream
- 1 tsp. salt
- 1/2 tsp. pepper
- 1/2 small onion, chopped
- 1 cup corn flake crumbs
- 2 Tbl. butter, melted

Direction

- Place frozen potatoes into a 9x13 buttered baking dish and add the cheddar cheese.
- Heat together margarine, chicken soup, sour cream, salt, pepper and onion.
- Melt the butter and mix with the crushed corn flake crumbs.
- Pour over the potato/cheese mixture and top with the corn flakes and butter.
- Bake at 350 degrees for 45-60 minutes or until light golden brown.

226. Potato Wedges Recipe

Serving: 4 | Prep: | Cook: 40mins | Ready in:

Ingredients

- Crisco butter Spray
- black pepper
- seasoned salt
- chili powder
- Mrs Dash Fiesta lime seasoning
- Four potatoes Cut into Wedges

Direction

- Preheat the oven to 350 F
- Cut the potatoes into wedges
- Spray the non-stick baking sheet with the Crisco butter spray
- Place the wedges into a medium sized bowl
- Spray the potatoes with the Crisco butter spray and season to desired taste. Mix the potatoes to spread the seasoning.
- Place the potatoes on baking sheet and bake in oven for 35 Minutes
- Remove Potatoes from oven and serve with desired condiments.

227. Potato And Ham Bake Recipe

Serving: 6 | Prep: | Cook: 25mins | Ready in:

Ingredients

- 1kg potatoes, (and/or sweet potatoes/ pumpkin) thinly sliced
- 200g ham, chopped
- 35g sachet of French onion soup
- 300g extra light sour cream
- 1/2 cup water
- 1/4 cup chopped parsley
- 1/4 cup breadcrumbs or bran

- 1/2 cup grated parmesan cheese
- olive oilspray

Direction

- Preheat oven to 200deg C.
- Lightly grease an 8 cup capacity ovenproof dish.
- Bring a saucepan of water to the boil.
- Add potato slices and cook 5 mins; drain...
- Layer 1/3 potato slices into dish.
- Scatter with 1/3 of ham. Repeat layers finishing with the ham.
- Empty soup sachet into a bowl and stir in sour cream, water and parsley. Pour over potatoes.
- Combine breadcrumbs and cheese and scatter over the top.
- Spray well with oil spray, and bake 25 mins until golden and tender.
- Serve with salad and crusty bread!

228. Potatoes Baked With Creamy Eggs Recipe

Serving: 4 | Prep: | Cook: 50mins | Ready in:

Ingredients

- 2-1/2 tablespoons butter, melted
- 4 cups potatoes, cooked and diced,
- salt and pepper to taste
- 4 eggs, beaten
- 2 cups sour cream
- 3 Tbsp. chopped chives or spring onions
- I like to top this dish with crumbled crispy bacon after I have removed it from the oven.

Direction

- Preheat oven to 350°F.
- Drizzle butter into the bottom of an oven proof casserole dish.
- Add cooked potatoes and season with salt and pepper.
- Mix together, eggs and sour cream.
- Add chives/spring onions to the mixture and pour over potatoes.
- Cover and bake in a preheated 350°F oven for 50 minutes.

229. Potatoes Ham Bake Recipe

Serving: 4 | Prep: | Cook: 30mins | Ready in:

Ingredients

- 1 lb. yukon gold potatoes, sliced
- 1 8-oz. tub light cream cheese spread with chive and onion
- 3/4 cup milk
- 1/4 cup finely shredded parmesan cheese
- 1 Tbsp. snipped fresh tarragon or 1/2 tsp. dried tarragon, crushed
- 8 oz. cooked boneless ham, cut in bite-sized slices
- 1 lb. fresh asparagus spears, trimmed, cut in 2 to 3-inch pieces
- tarragon sprigs (optional)

Direction

- Preheat oven to 400 degrees F. In medium saucepan cook potatoes, covered, in small amount of lightly salted boiling water 5 to 7 minutes, just until tender. Drain; transfer to bowl and set aside.
- For sauce, in same saucepan combine cream cheese, milk, 2 tablespoons Parmesan, and 1/4 teaspoon black pepper. Heat and whisk until smooth and cheese is melted. Remove from heat; stir in tarragon.
- Layer potatoes, ham, asparagus, and sauce in 1-1/2-quart baking dish. Bake, covered, 20 minutes. Uncover; sprinkle remaining Parmesan. Bake 10 to 12 minutes. Let stand 5 minutes. Top with tarragon and freshly ground black pepper.

230. Quick Fake Baked Potatos With Crispy Skin Recipe

Serving: 1 | Prep: | Cook: 16mins | Ready in:

Ingredients

- potato or other vegetables
- butter
- salt
- pepper
- granulated onion
- sour cream
- chives and whatever else you like

Direction

- I love a good cooked (almost baked for real) potato and for a crispy skin here is what I do instead of waiting an hour. I use this when I don't have time to wait for a "real" baked potato.
- Rinse the potato with water, pierce the skin with a fork in couple of places and place in a Seal-a-Meal bag.
- Cook 1 potato for 6 minutes, 2 may take 8 minutes depending on your microwave. Each potato should yield to finger pressure and then it is done.
- Carefully remove bag from Microwave, full of steam and hot potatoes.
- Rub the potato with olive oil and place on your hot BBQ grill for about 10 minutes. I will let it cook about 4 minutes, put on a couple of rib eye steak (1/2" thick) and these cook 3 minutes per side over a high open flame. Just awesome.
- Turn a couple of times to prevent burning and you have a cooked potato with a crispy skin in 16 minutes (microwave and grill). Not exactly like a true baked potato cooked for 50-60 minutes, but I won't throw it off the plate. I take about 10 minutes fixing my potato. I use the fork to break all the potato from the skin then start mixing in real butter. Once it all mixed down to skin, I season with salt, pepper and granulated onion and mix well. No dry potato. Sour cream can be added, chives and whatever you like. I find the salt, pepper and onion powder to me pretty dang good and tasty.
- Or just cook them in the bag and eat. Whatever you like. Yes, cooked in the bag after rising they will steam and be soft skinned, so for crispy skins, BBQ grill.
- The skin is full of vitamins, and a crunchy skin with butter, salt and pepper and other fillings and rolled up like a Taquitos is killer good.
- Ok this is cool thing I learned long ago, original, well I am an inventor by trade.
- The Seal-A-Meal bag is made of a special plastic, you can cook veggies in it over and over without harming the bag. It is virtually indestructible.
- If you don't own the Sealing machine, you can still buy a roll or
- Pre-made bags in most Ace stores or look online. Every kitchen should have these bags.
- They work so well. I make my bags about 18 inches long so I can put stuff in, fold it over and place the folded part down, being held by the stuff.
- There you go, a kitchen trade secret exposed to the world. JJ

231. Re Baked Potatoes Recipe

Serving: 6 | Prep: | Cook: 90mins | Ready in:

Ingredients

- 6 baking potatoes
- 6 tbsp butter
- 3/4 cup of milk or Cream
- 1-1/2 tsp salt
- 3//8 tsp black pepper
- 3/4 tsp garlic powder
- 1-1/2 cup Shredded cheddar cheese
- green onion tops or Chves

- 3 strips of bacon, fried crisp and crumbled

Direction

- Rub potatoes with oil and bake at 450 for about 1-1/2 hours. Or until a fork easily penetrates to the centre.
- Cut baked potatoes in half. Cut them so they will lay flat as halves.
- Scoop out the centre of the potatoes with a spoon leaving 1/4 inch of potato meat around the edges.
- Mash the potato pulp and combine with warm milk, garlic powder, salt, pepper and butter. Blend with a mixer until smooth.
- Place potato shells in a baking dish large enough to hold them in a single layer. Fill with the potato mixture.
- Top with onion/chive, bacon and shredded cheese.
- Microwave or broil until cheese is melted and mixture is heated through.

232. Reuben Baked Potatoes Recipe

Serving: 8 | Prep: | Cook: 70mins | Ready in:

Ingredients

- 4 large paking potatoes
- 2 c finely diced cooked corned beef
- 1 can sauerkraut(14 oz)rinsed,well drained and finely chopped
- 1/2 c shredded swiss cheese
- 3 Tbs sliced green onions
- 1 garlic clove,minced
- 1 Tbs prepared horseradish
- 1 tsp caraway seeds
- 1 pkg (3oz) cream cheese,softened
- 3 Tbs grated parmesan cheese

Direction

- Bake potatoes at 425 for 45 mins. Or till tender. Cool. In a bowl, combine the corned beef, sauerkraut, Swiss cheese, onions, garlic, horseradish and caraway. Cut potatoes in half lengthwise. Carefully scoop out potatoes, leaving shells intact.
- Mash potatoes with cream cheese; stir in corned beef mixture. Mound potato mixture into the shells. Sprinkle with parmesan cheese and paprika. Return to the oven for 25 mins or till heated through.

233. Roasted Cajun Potatoes Recipe

Serving: 8 | Prep: | Cook: 75mins | Ready in:

Ingredients

- 2-1/2 pounds medium red potatoes
- 1/4 cup olive oil
- 2 shallots, chopped
- 1 garlic clove, minced
- 1 teaspoon salt
- 1/2 teaspoon paprika
- 1/2 teaspoon cayenne pepper
- 1/2 teaspoon pepper
- 2 tablespoons minced fresh parsley

Direction

- Cut each potato lengthwise into eight wedges. In a large bowl, combine the oil, shallots, garlic, salt, paprika, cayenne and pepper; add potatoes and toss to coat. Place in greased roasting pan.
- Bake, uncovered, at 450° for 45-50 minutes or until tender and golden brown, turning every 15 minutes. Sprinkle with parsley.

234. Rosemary Garlic Garnished Baked Potatoes Recipe

Serving: 2 | Prep: | Cook: 30mins | Ready in:

Ingredients

- 4 potatoes
- 2 Steams of Fresh rosemary
- 2 garlic heads chopped
- peppercorn medley to taste
- salt to taste
- Red Crushed Pepper (Optional)

Direction

- Cut Potatoes in half then slice in wedges about 5-6 per potato.
- Place them in an oiled baking tray.
- Cover with rosemary, chopped garlic, peppercorn, red pepper and salt. Pour olive oil over it.
- Serve topped with, Sour Cream and fresh green onions and pastured-grazed white cheddar.
- I use "Benissimo" Mediterranean garlic olive oil.
- I served this as a side for vegetarian chili over rice.

235. Ruben Stuffed Baked Potatoes Recipe

Serving: 4 | Prep: | Cook: 75mins | Ready in:

Ingredients

- 4 large baking potatoes
- 2 cups corned beef, finely diced
- 1 bag sauerkraut, rinsed and drained
- 1/2-1 cup shredded swiss cheese
- 3 tablespoons scallions, diced
- 1 tablespoon horseradish
- 1 clove garlic, minced
- 1 package cream cheese, softened
- 3 tablespoons parmesan cheese
- paprika

Direction

- Bake potatoes at 425° for 45 minutes, or until tender.
- Cool.
- In a bowl, combine corned beef, sauerkraut, Swiss cheese, scallions, garlic and horseradish.
- Cut potatoes in half lengthwise. Carefully scoop out potatoes, leaving just the skins of the potatoes intact.
- In a bowl, mash potatoes with cream cheese.
- Stir in the corned beef mixture.
- Mound potato mixture into the skins of the potatoes.
- Sprinkle with parmesan cheese and paprika.
- Return to the oven for 30 minutes more, or until heated all the way through.

236. Salmon Stuffed Baked Potatoes Recipe

Serving: 4 | Prep: | Cook: 75mins | Ready in:

Ingredients

- 4 large baking potatoes
- 1 7 1/2 oz can salmon
- 1/2 c sour cream
- 1/4 c chopped sharp cheddar cheese
- 1 tbsp chopped green onion
- 1 tbsp chopped dill
- 1 tbsp lemon juice
- 1/2 tsp hot pepper sauce
- sea salt, pepper and smoked paprika to taste
- 1/3 c shredded cheddar

Direction

- Scrub potatoes, prick potatoes and bake in a 400 F oven for 45 to 55 minutes or until tender when gently squeezed

- In bowl, combine salmon, sour cream, diced cheese, onion, dill, lemon juice and hot pepper sauce.
- Season to taste with salt, pepper and smoked paprika
- Cut a 1/2 in thick slice from top of each potato
- Scoop out pulp, leaving a 1/4 in shell
- Mash pulp and stir into salmon mixture
- Spoon into potato shells
- Top with shredded cheddar
- Bake at 400F for 15-20 minutes until tops are crisp

237. Salt Baked Potatoes With Roasted Garlic Butter Recipe

Serving: 4 | Prep: | Cook: 2hours | Ready in:

Ingredients

- 2-12 c plus 1/8 tsp(can use Kosher or table salt)
- 4 russet potatoes,scrubbed and dried
- 1 whole head garlic,outer skin removed and top 1/4 of head cut off
- 4 tsp olive oil
- 4 TB unsalted butter

Direction

- 1. Adjust oven rack to middle and heat oven to 450'. Spread 2-1/2 c salt in even layer in 13x9" bake dish. Gently nestle potatoes in salt, broad side down, leaving space between potatoes. Add garlic, cut side up to baking dish. Cover dish with foil and crimp edges to tightly seal. Bake 1-1/4 hours; remove pan from oven. Increase temp to 500'.
- 2. Carefully remove foil from dish...Remove garlic and set aside to cool. Brush exposed portion of each potato with 1 tsp. oil. Return uncovered baking dish to oven and bake till potatoes are tender when pierced with tip of paring knife and skins are glossy,15 to 20 mins.
- 3. Meanwhile, once garlic is cool enough to handle, squeeze root end until cloves slip out of skins. Using for, mash garlic, butter 1/8 tsp. kosher salt (or pinch table salt) to smooth paste. Remove any clumped salt from potatoes, split lengthwise, top with portion of butter and serve immediately...Yummy!

238. Sausage Stuffed Baked Potatoes Recipe

Serving: 4 | Prep: | Cook: 180mins | Ready in:

Ingredients

- 2 leftover baked baking potatoes, OR 2 unbaked (must be baked for one hour)
- cooking time is reduced if using leftover potatoes
- 1 tbsp extra virgin olive oil
- 2 mild Italian sausages, removed from the casing
- 1 small onion, finely chopped
- 4 cloves fresh garlic, finely chopped
- ½ tsp Italian herb seasoning
- ½ tsp crushed fennel seeds
- 1 sweet red pepper, diced
- 2 tbsp fresh Italian parsley, finely chopped
- ¼ tsp salt
- ¾ cup shredded asiago cheese
- 1 egg
- salt and pepper to taste

Direction

- Cut the potatoes in half lengthwise
- Scoop out the inside with a spoon and reserve in a bowl
- Place the potato shells on a baking sheet
- Preheat the oven to 400*F
- Heat the oil over medium high heat
- Add the sausage, onion, garlic, herb seasoning and fennel seeds

- Cook mixture about 8 minutes, breaking up any lumps, and until no pink is seen in the meat
- Add the parsley and salt
- Let this mixture cool slightly
- Stir into this ½ cup Asiago cheese and egg
- Combine thoroughly
- Spoon this mixture into the potato shells
- Sprinkle each with the remaining cheese
- Bake about 30 minutes, or until golden brown.

239. Savory Potato Bake Dated 1962 Recipe

Serving: 10 | Prep: | Cook: 50mins | Ready in:

Ingredients

- 1 cup ricotta cheese
- 1/2 cup soft whole grain or white bread crumbs
- 1 tablespoon chopped fresh or 1 teaspoon dried marjoram leaves
- 1/2 teaspoon salt
- 1/4 teaspoon pepper
- 3 egg whites
- 4 cups shredded sweet potatoes
- 4 cups shredded potatoes
- 3/4 cup chopped onion
- 2 cups applesauce
- 1/4 cup sour cream

Direction

- Preheat oven to 375.
- Spray rectangular pan with non-stick cooking spray.
- Mix cheese, bread crumbs, marjoram, salt, pepper and egg whites in large bowl.
- Stir in potatoes and onion then spread in pan and bake 45 minutes.
- Serve with applesauce and sour cream.

240. Scampi Baked Potato Recipe

Serving: 4 | Prep: | Cook: 75mins | Ready in:

Ingredients

- 1 tbls. olive oil
- 2 baking potatoes
- 8 medium-large shrimp, peeled and deveined
- salt and pepper, to taste
- 4 tbls. parmesan cheese, grated
- garlic butter
- 1 tbls. olive oil
- 1 small shallot, finely chopped
- 1 large clove garlic, finely chopped
- 1 tbls. chives, finely chopped
- 1 tbls. parsley, finely chopped
- 1 stick butter, softened
- salt and pepper, to taste

Direction

- Preheat oven to 350
- Wash potatoes
- Poke holes with a fork into potato
- Bake for about 45 minutes or until potato is tender
- Garlic butter
- Heat olive oil in a medium pan
- Add shallot and garlic and sauté until tender
- Remove from the heat and cool
- In mixing bowl, mix butter, shallot and garlic, and herbs
- Season with salt and pepper
- Cut warm potatoes in 1/2
- Scoop out potato to 1/4 in. with a spoon
- Put excess potatoes in a bowl and keep warm
- Put shrimp in the potato boat in a layer
- Spoon 1-1 1/2 tbsp. garlic butter over shrimp
- Add remaining butter to saved potato and mix together
- Put over shrimp in a mound
- Sprinkle Parmesan cheese over potato
- Return to oven and bake until heated through and cheese makes a golden crust, about 20 minutes

241. Shake N Bake Potatos Recipe

Serving: 6 | Prep: | Cook: 60mins | Ready in:

Ingredients

- 10-12 medium gold/red, or 8-10 large russet potatos
- 1/4 cup olive oil
- 1/8 cup *Durkee Garden Seasoning*
- garlic salt
- rosemary
- fresh ground black pepper

Direction

- Cut potatoes into 2' wedges, or cube 1-2" put in large bowl with tight fitting lid, or 1 gallon Ziploc bag
- Add olive oil, *Durkee Garden Seasoning*
- Shake shake shake until potatoes are coated with oil and seasoning is evenly distributed
- Place potatoes in large baking dish or pan (coat with non-stick spray)
- Sprinkle with garlic salt, rosemary, and ground black pepper
- Bake at 450 for 1 hour or until browned, stirring occasionally

242. Sliced Baked Potatoes Microwaved Recipe

Serving: 4 | Prep: | Cook: 15mins | Ready in:

Ingredients

- 4 medium (same size)potatoes
- 1 tsp. salt
- 3 Tbs. melted margarine
- 3 Tbs. Herbs: parsley, chives, thyme, sage or other
- 3 tsp. dried herbs of your choice
- 2/3 cup shredded cheddar cheese
- 1 ½ Tbs. parmesan cheese

Direction

- 1) Potatoes: peel if skin is tough, otherwise just rinse and pat dry.
- 2) Cut potatoes into thin slices, but not all the way through. Use a handle of a spoon to prevent knife from cutting all the way.
- 3) Place potatoes in a micro-safe dish or pan. Sprinkle with melted margarine and chopped parsley, chives, or other herbs.
- 4) Microwave at HIGH power for 10 minutes, rearranging the potatoes after 5 minutes.
- 5) Let rest for 5 minutes.
- 6) Sprinkle with shredded cheddar and Parmesan cheese.
- 7) Microwave for another 4 to 6 minutes at HIGH power until cheeses are melted and potatoes are soft. Sprinkle with salt if desired or sprinkle with shredded Cheddar for a more cheesy potato.
- 8) Serve potatoes as a side dish or as a main dish with just a salad.

243. Sliced Baked Potatoes Recipe

Serving: 4 | Prep: | Cook: 65mins | Ready in:

Ingredients

- 4 medium potatoes,pared
- 1tsp.salt
- 4Tbs. melted butter
- 3Tbs.chopped parsley or chives
- 4Tbs grated cheddar cheese
- 2Tbs. parmesan cheese.

Direction

- Cut potatoes in thin slices but not all the way thru. Put potatoes in a baking dish and fan them out slightly. Sprinkle with salt and drizzle each with the melted butter. Sprinkle with the herbs. Bake in a preheated 425 oven for about 50 mins. Remove from oven. Sprinkle with the cheeses.
- Return to oven and bake another 10-15 mins until lightly browned and cheeses are melted and potatoes are soft.

244. Slow Cooker Cheesy Tuna Baked Potatoes Recipe

Serving: 4 | Prep: | Cook: 300mins | Ready in:

Ingredients

- 4 medium Idaho or russet potatoes, scrubbed and left dripping wet
- 3/4 cup finely shredded cheddar, divided
- 1/4 cup milk
- 1 can (6oz) tuna, drained
- 1/2 cup sour cream (low fat is fine)
- 1 green onion (white & some green) thinly sliced

Direction

- Prick each potato with a fork or the tip of a knife and pile into the slow cooker. Do not add water.
- Cover and cook until fork-tender, on HIGH for 3 to 5 hours, or LOW 6 to 8 hours.
- Remove from the cooker with tongs and cut in half lengthwise.
- Scoop out the centre of each half, leaving enough potato to keep the shell intact.
- Put the potato flesh into a bowl & add a half cup of the cheese, the milk, tuna, sour cream, and green onion.
- Mash the filling with a fork and spoon it back into the shells, mounding it high.
- Return to the slow cooker, setting them down in a single layer, if possible so they touch each other.
- Sprinkle with the remaining 1/4 cup cheese.
- Cover and cook on HIGH for 45 minutes to 1 hour.
- Remove carefully from the cooker and serve immediately.

245. Smashed Potatoes A Flip On Baked Potatoes Recipe

Serving: 4 | Prep: | Cook: 15mins | Ready in:

Ingredients

- 4 potatoes
- extra virgin olive oil
- salt
- pepper
- garlic powder
- caraway seeds
- (use your favorite seasonings, BUT def try the caraway!!!!!)

Direction

- Cook potatoes in microwave if using fresh
- Preheat oven to 400 F
- Line cookie sheet with foil
- Drizzle evoo on foil
- Sprinkle with some of the seasonings
- Take a potato and place on mixture then Smoosh with a salad plate (until about 1/2"-1" thick)
- Repeat with rest of potatoes
- Drizzle some more evoo on top of potatoes and sprinkle with some more seasonings
- Bake for approx. 15 minutes
- Potatoes should be crunchy and golden on the outside but smooth and creamy on the inside ENJOY!

246. Smoked 'taters Recipe

Serving: 6 | Prep: | Cook: 3hours | Ready in:

Ingredients

- 6 large Russet Potatoes (or 1 for each person eating).
- Olive Oil
- Coarse Kosher Salt

Direction

- Wash Potatoes and score each across the top 5 or 6 times with a sharp knife. The scores don't need to be too deep, skin just needs to be cut through
- Take a bowl or deep platter and pour a 1/4 cup or so of Olive Oil in.
- To that, add a good amount of Kosher Salt, 2-3 TBS or more depending on the number of Potatoes, you should have a pretty thick mix.
- Roll each of the Potatoes in the oil and salt making sure they are well covered, I normally rub the spuds around in my hands.
- Place score side up in your smoker, or however you smoke your meats, at about 225 - 275 degrees F for around 2-3 hours or until they are tender to the touch. Time will vary depending on size of Potatoes and temperature you are smoking at.
- Serve hot with Butter, fresh chopped chives and sour cream. Enjoy!!!

247. Smoked Cheese Filler For Baked Potato Recipe

Serving: 0 | Prep: | Cook: 10mins | Ready in:

Ingredients

- Smoked cheese
- spring onion
- A little bit of garlic
- Fresh dill
- And some dried mushrooms

Direction

- Actually you can just mix all the ingredients in to the base potato mass, makes a great appetizer for any kind of meal.

248. Smoked Fish Filler For Baked Potato Recipe

Serving: 0 | Prep: | Cook: 10mins | Ready in:

Ingredients

- Smoked fish
- spring onion
- Cream + mayo

Direction

- Cut the fish in to small chunks
- Cover in mayo and cream souse adding chopped spring onion tales
- Add on top of the potato and feel nasty.

249. Special Baked Potatoes Recipe

Serving: 4 | Prep: | Cook: 90mins | Ready in:

Ingredients

- 4 medium baking potatoes (I prefer russets)
- 1/2 cup sour cream
- salt and pepper to taste
- Sliced green onion tops

Direction

- Bake potatoes by your preferred method of baking potatoes then let them cool until you can handle them.

- Cut a slice from the top of each potato.
- On your slices, carefully peel off the skin and discard. Place the potato slices in a bowl.
- Use a spoon to carefully scoop the potato out of the inside of your baked potatoes, just leaving a thin shell of potato and peel.
- Add the potato you scoop out to the potato slices in the bowl and set aside your potato shells.
- Mash the potato in the bowl.
- Beat in sour cream, salt and pepper until fluffy.
- Divide mixture between potato shells.
- Place filled potatoes in an 11x7 baking dish.
- Bake at 425 for 20 to 25 minutes, until heated all the way through.
- Top with green onion tops.
- You may make these ahead of time and refrigerate. If you do, add 10 minutes to baking time.

250. Spiced Baked Potatoes Recipe

Serving: 4 | Prep: | Cook: 70mins | Ready in:

Ingredients

- 4 russet potatoes
- 1-2 Tbs butter
- 1/2-1 tsp pumpkin pie spice

Direction

- Bake the potatoes at 400-425 degrees for an hour. Cut in half lengthwise. Melt butter and sprinkle potatoes with pumpkin pie spice. Sauté till potatoes are browned.

251. Spinach Mashed Potatoes Recipe

Serving: 10 | Prep: | Cook: 65mins | Ready in:

Ingredients

- 3 pounds potatoes, peeled and quartered
- 1 cup (8 ounces) sour cream
- 1/2 cup butter
- 1 teaspoon sugar
- 1 teaspoon salt
- 1/2 teaspoon pepper
- 1/4 to 1/2 teaspoon dill weed
- 1 package (10 ounces) frozen chopped spinach, thawed and drained
- 1/3 cup shredded cheddar cheese

Direction

- Place the potatoes in a saucepan and cover with water; cover and bring to a boil over medium-high heat. Cook for 15-20 minutes or until very tender. Drain well and place in a mixing bowl; mash. Add the sour cream, butter, sugar, salt, pepper and dill; mix well. Stir in spinach.
- Transfer to a greased 2-qt. baking dish. Sprinkle with cheese. Bake, uncovered, at 350° for 30-35 minutes or cheese is melted.

252. Spinach Potato Cakes Recipe

Serving: 0 | Prep: | Cook: 20mins | Ready in:

Ingredients

- Ingredients:
- 2 lbs yukon gold potatoes, diced -
- 1/2 cup extra virgin olive oil -
- 1/4 cup onion, diced -
- 2 tsp garlic, minced -
- 1 tsp rosemary, fresh or dried -
- 10 1/2 oz frozen spinach, thawed & chopped -

- 1 cup feta, crumbled -
- 1/2 cup Parmesan, grated -
- 2 eggs -
- 1 tsp oregano, dried -
- 1/2 tsp sea salt -
- 1 tsp Freshly ground black pepper -
- 1 1/2 cups bread crumbs

Direction

- 1. Steam or boil potatoes until soft. Mash and set aside to cool
- 2. In a large skillet over medium heat, cook onions and garlic in oil until soft (about 10 minutes). Set aside to cool.
- 3. In a large bowl, combine cooled potatoes, onion mix and all remaining ingredients until well mixed. Scoop or form mixture into 3/4-inch patties.
- 4. Pan-fry patties in a small amount of oil on medium heat for a minute on each side to create a crust.
- 5. Place on baking sheet and bake in a preheated 350°F oven for 15-20 minutes. Remove from oven and enjoy hot.
- Yields 12 Cakes

253. Spinach And Cheese Baked Potatoes Recipe

Serving: 4 | Prep: | Cook: 75mins | Ready in:

Ingredients

- 4 baking potatoes scrubbed
- 8 cups loosely packed spinach
- 1 tablespoon olive oil
- 1 small onion finely chopped
- 1/2 cup ricotta cheese
- 1 pinch grated nutmeg
- 1/2 teaspoon salt
- 1 teaspoon freshly ground black pepper

Direction

- Prick potatoes all over with a fork then bake at 425 for 1-1/4 hours.
- Wash spinach and put into saucepan with only the water remaining on the leaves.
- Cook over low heat for 2 minutes until spinach has just wilted.
- Drain thoroughly squeezing to remove excess water then chop spinach finely.
- Heat olive oil in saucepan then add onion and cook gently stirring occasionally 5 minutes.
- Cut potatoes in half lengthwise then scoop out flesh and transfer to a bowl.
- Add spinach, onion, any oil left in pan, ricotta, nutmeg, salt and pepper and mix thoroughly.
- Fill potato skins with mixture then return to oven and cook 20 minutes then serve immediately.

254. Stuffed Baked Sweet Potatoes Recipe

Serving: 6 | Prep: | Cook: 70mins | Ready in:

Ingredients

- 6 medium orange fleshed sweet potatoes
- 1/2 cup orange juice
- 3 tablespoons butter
- 1 teaspoon salt
- 8 ounce can crushed drained pineapple
- 1/2 cup chopped pecans

Direction

- Bake potatoes at 375 for 1 hour.
- Cut a 1 inch lengthwise strip from top of each potato and scoop pulp from shell.
- Combine pulp, orange juice, butter and salt then gently stir in pineapple.
- Stuff shells with mixture and sprinkle with pecans.
- Bake at 375 for 10 minutes.

255. Stuffed Potato Skins Recipe

Serving: 4 | Prep: | Cook: 10mins | Ready in:

Ingredients

- 8 small floury potatoes - such a Maris Pipers
- 1 tbsp vegetable oil1 tbsp vegetable oil
- 7 oz (200g) pancetta cubes (or bacon lardons)7 oz (200g) pancetta cubes (or bacon lardons)
- 2 tbsp double/heavy cream2 tbsp double/heavy cream
- 2 tbsp salted butter2 tbsp salted butter
- 1 pinch of salt and pepper1 pinch of salt and pepper
- 1 3/4 cups (175g) of your favourite cheese - I used a mix of 75% mature chedder and 25% red Leicester, grated1 3/4 cups (175g) of your favourite cheese - I used a mix of 75% mature chedder and 25% red Leicester, grated
- 4 tbsp soured cream4 tbsp soured cream
- 4 spring onions (scallions) - chopped4 spring onions (scallions) - chopped

Direction

- Preheat your oven to 190c. Prick your potatoes with a fork and start them off in the microwave. Put all the potatoes in the microwave and microwave on high for 10 minutes (alternatively you can add 20 minutes to the cooking time in the oven).
- Put your potatoes in the oven, directly on the shelf and cook for 35-45 minutes until they're crisp on the outside and soft on the inside (you can check this by stabbing a knife into one of the potatoes to see if it slides in easily).
- Meanwhile, heat the oil in a small frying pan/skillet over a medium-high heat. Cook the pancetta cubes for 5-6 minutes, until crispy. Remove from the pan.
- When your potatoes are ready, take out of the oven and chop each of the potatoes in half. Pick up a potato half (using a tea towel to protect your hands) and using a spoon, scoop out the insides into a large bowl. Repeat with the rest of the potatoes.
- Add the cream, butter and salt & pepper to the bowl and mash using a potato masher or a fork until the potato is fluffy.
- Add in the pancetta and cheese (reserving a small handful for sprinkling on top). Mix together.
- Take one of the potato skins and put a spoonful of the potato mix inside. Put the potato in a baking dish and sprinkle with a little of the reserved cheese. Repeat with the remaining potatoes.
- When all of the potatoes are stuffed, put them back in the oven for 10-15 minutes (same temperature).
- Take out of the oven and serve with soured cream and a sprinkling of spring onions (scallions).

256. Sweet Potato Apple Bake Recipe

Serving: 4 | Prep: | Cook: 10mins | Ready in:

Ingredients

- 1 large cooking apple peeled and quartered
- 2 cups mashed sweet potatoes
- 2 eggs separated at room temperature
- 1/2 teaspoon vanilla extract
- vegetable cooking spray
- 1-1/2 teaspoons margarine
- apple slices
- lemon juice

Direction

- Place apple quarters in a saucepan then cover with water and bring to a boil.
- Reduce heat and simmer 8 minutes then drain well.
- Position knife blade in food processor bowl and add apples.
- Top with cover and process until smooth.

- Combine apples, sweet potatoes, egg yolks and vanilla then stir well and set aside.
- Beat egg whites until peaks are stiff but not dry then fold into sweet potato mixture.
- Pour mixture into a 1 quart casserole coated with cooking spray then dot with margarine and bake at 350 for 45 minutes.
- Garnish with apple slices dipped in lemon juice if desired.

257. Sweet Potato Bake Recipe

Serving: 6 | Prep: | Cook: 40mins | Ready in:

Ingredients

- 2 medium sweet potatoes, thinly sliced
- 1 clove of garlic, crushed
- 1/2 tsp finely grated nutmeg
- 1 cup grated cheddar
- 1 tsp finely chopped rosemary
- 1 cup cream

Direction

- Preheat oven to 180 C (350F)
- Place potatoes in layers in a baking pan
- Sprinkle evenly with other ingredients and pour over the cream
- Bake for 35-40 minutes or until tender

258. Sweet Potato Berry Bake Recipe

Serving: 8 | Prep: | Cook: 35mins | Ready in:

Ingredients

- 2 cans sweet potatoes halves, drained (17 oz Size)
- 1 cup cranberries
- 1/4 cup chopped pecans
- 1/2 cup orange marmalade
- 1 1/2 cups miniature marshmellows

Direction

- Arrange sweet potatoes in a 10 x 6 inch baking dish.
- Top with cranberries and nuts.
- Dot with marmalade.
- Bake at 350 degrees for 30 to 35 minutes.
- Sprinkle with marshmallows.
- Broil until lightly brown.

259. Sweet Potato Pineapple Bake Recipe

Serving: 6 | Prep: | Cook: 35mins | Ready in:

Ingredients

- 2 (15 oz) cans sweet potatoes, drained
- 1 (8oz) can crushed pineapple in juice, do not drain
- 1/2 tsp cinnamon
- 1/4 cup raisins
- 1/4 cup chopped pecans (I used walnuts)
- 1 cup mini marshmallows

Direction

- Cut potatoes into small pieces and place in a large bowl.
- Add remaining ingredients (except marshmallows), toss to mix
- Lightly oil a deep dish pie pan and place potato mixture in pan. Top with marshmallows.
- Bake uncovered at 350 degrees for 35 minutes, or until mixture bubbles at the edges and the top is browned.

260. Sweet Potatoes In Crockpot Recipe

Serving: 4 | Prep: | Cook: 4hours | Ready in:

Ingredients

- 2 pounds sweet potatoes, peeled and cubed
- 1/2 cup packed dark brown sugar
- 1/2 cup butter, cut into small pieces
- 1 teaspoon ground cinnamon
- 1/2 teaspoon ground nutmeg
- 1 medium orange, juiced
- 1/4 teaspoon salt
- 1 teaspoon vanilla
- toasted chopped pecans

Direction

- Place sweet potatoes in bottom of slow cooker.
- Mix spices and orange juice together.
- Stir into sweet potatoes.
- Cook on High for 2 hours or on Low for 4 hours.
- Check for doneness because each crockpot cooks at a different heat setting.
- Before serving, stir in toasted pecans.

261. Taco Tater Skins Recipe

Serving: 12 | Prep: | Cook: 80mins | Ready in:

Ingredients

- 6 large russet potatoes
- 1/2 cup butter, melted
- 2 tablespoons taco seasoning
- 1 cup (4 ounces) shredded cheddar cheese
- 15 bacon strips, cooked and crumbled
- 3 green onions, chopped
- salsa and/or sour cream, optional

Direction

- Bake potatoes at 375° for 1 hour or until tender. Reduce heat to
- 350°. When cool enough to handle, cut the potatoes lengthwise into quarters. Scoop out pulp, leaving a 1/4-in. shell (save pulp for another use).
- Combine the butter and taco seasoning; brush over both sides of potato skins. Place skin side down on a greased baking sheet.
- Sprinkle with cheese, bacon and onions.
- Bake for 5-10 minutes or until the cheese is melted. Serve with salsa and/or sour cream if desired.

262. The Best Sour Cream Your Baked Potato Will Ever Meet Recipe

Serving: 1 | Prep: | Cook: 15mins | Ready in:

Ingredients

- 1 1/2 lb. mushrooms, chopped
- 1/2 onion, chopped (I've also used shallots)
- 2 cloves garlic, chopped
- 1 cup sour cream
- 1 tbls. soy sauce
- salt and pepper to taste
- chives, chopped to garnish
- olive oil to saute vegetables

Direction

- Heat oil over medium heat
- Sauté onion a minute or 2
- Add garlic and mushrooms and sauté for about 10 minutes
- Cool
- Add to food processor and pulse until smooth.
- Add sour cream, soy sauce, and salt and pepper and pulse to blend
- If serving over potatoes, garnish with chives
- If using for dip, add 1 roma tomato, seeded and chopped then garnish with chives

263. Tiny Baked New Potatoes Recipe

Serving: 6 | Prep: | Cook: 60mins | Ready in:

Ingredients

- 2 pounds (1 kilo) of the tiniest new potatoes you can find
- olive oil the best you can get
- 1-2 pounds coarse salt Kosher or pickling salt

Direction

- Preheat the oven to 400°F or 200°C
- Wash the potatoes well and dry them
- Coat your hands with a bit of olive oil and then rub the potatoes so they are lightly coated.
- Put a thin layer of the salt into a baking dish-- I use a soufflé dish--then a layer of potatoes, cover with salt, more potatoes, until the dish is filled with salt covered potatoes.
- Tuck the dish into the hot oven and bake them for up to one hour-- it may take less, so try them beginning at 35 minutes. They will be soft to a squeeze when they are done.
- Take the potatoes out of the oven and using paper towels, remove the excess salt. When the salt is cooled, you can store it in a bag to use the next time.
- The salt holds even heat against all surfaces of the potatoes and also removes excess water as they cook.

264. Tuna Baked Potatoes Recipe

Serving: 4 | Prep: | Cook: 60mins | Ready in:

Ingredients

- 2 cans tuna, drained
- 4 baking potatoes, cleaned
- 1/2 c. milk
- 1/4 c. butter
- 1/2 c. parmesan cheese, grated
- 1/4 c. green onion, minced
- 1 tsp. thyme
- 1 tsp. dill
- 1 tsp. salt
- 1 tsp. pepper
- 1/4 c. frozen peas, thawed

Direction

- Bake potatoes. When cool, cut in half and scoop out centers. Mash potatoes and beat in cheese, onion and spices. Stir tuna and peas. Spoon mixture back into hollowed out skins. Bake at 350 degrees for 20 minutes.

265. Turkey Potato Bake Recipe

Serving: 6 | Prep: | Cook: 40mins | Ready in:

Ingredients

- 3 cups hot mashed potatoes
- 1 cup shredded cheese
- 1 can fried onions
- 1 1/2 cups shredded turkey
- 1 pkg frozen peas and carrots
- 1 can cream of chicken soup
- 1/2 cup milk
- 1/2 tsp dry mustard
- 1/4 tsp garlic powder
- 1/4 tsp pepper

Direction

- Combine potatoes, 1/2 cup cheese, and 1/2 cup fried onions.
- Spoon into a greased 1 1/2 quart casserole dish, spread across bottom and up the sides of the dish.

- Combine the next 7 ingredients. Pour into potato shell.
- Bake uncovered at 375 degrees for 30 minutes.
- Top with remaining cheese and onions.
- Bake for additional 5-10 minutes
- Let stand 10-15 minutes before serving.

266. Tuscan Cheese Potato Bake Recipe

Serving: 10 | Prep: | Cook: 30mins | Ready in:

Ingredients

- 2 lbs red potatoes
- 3 or 4 cloves garlic, minced
- 1-1/2 tsp snipped fresh thyme or 1/2 tsp dried thyme
- 1/4 c butter
- 1 c buttermilk
- 4 oz. Fontina cheese, shredded (1 c)
- 4 oz. parmesan cheese, finely shredded (1 c)
- 1/3 c crumbled blue cheese
- 1/2 c panko
- 1/4 tsp dried Italian seasoning
- 1 Tbs olive oil
- snipped fresh parsley (optional)

Direction

- Preheat oven to 400. Lightly grease a 2 qt. square baking dish; set aside. Scrub potatoes; cut in 1" pieces. In large saucepan, cook potatoes in lightly salted boiling water 12 to 15 mins. Or till tender; drain.
- In 12" skillet, cook and stir garlic and thyme in butter over med. heat 1 minded potatoes. Coarsely mash potatoes. Stir in buttermilk, 1/2 tsp. salt and 1/4 tsp. pepper. Fold in fontina cheese, half of the parmesan and the blue cheese. Evenly spread in baking dish.
- In small bowl, combine remaining Parmesan, panko, Italian seasoning and oil; toss with fork to combine. Evenly sprinkle over potato mixture in dish. Bake 20 mins or till bubbly and top is golden. Sprinkle with snipped parsley.

267. Two Potatoe Baked Cassarole Recipe

Serving: 8 | Prep: | Cook: 80mins | Ready in:

Ingredients

- 5-6 potatoes peeled and sliced thin
- 1 large sweet potatoe peeld and sliced thin
- 1 jar of Ragu Double cheddar cheese sauce
- 1 can cream of celery soup
- 1 can cream of potatoe soup
- 1 large onion diced
- fresh broccolli cut up small (as desired)
- garlic powder (as desired)
- white ground pepper (as desired)
- garlic salt
- 2 fresh pressed garlic cloves

Direction

- Peel and slice all potatoes, rinse well with cold water and set aside to drain well.
- In a large bowl mix all soups and cheese sauce and spices
- Add diced onions and stir well.
- Add potatoes and toss well to coat all potatoes.
- Pour into casserole dishes and bake for 80 minutes on 350.
- Top with French onions and bake for 5 - 10 minutes more.
- Let cool for a bit and serve.

268. Ukranaian Potato Bake Dated 1967 Recipe

Serving: 8 | Prep: | Cook: 50mins | Ready in:

Ingredients

- 1/4 pound sliced bacon, diced
- 2 large white onions finely chopped
- 3 pounds new potatoes peeled
- 1 cup light cream
- 3 large egg yolks slightly beaten
- 1 teaspoon salt
- 2 teaspoons freshly ground black pepper
- 2 large egg whites
- 4 tablespoons unsalted butter

Direction

- Sauté bacon in a medium skillet over medium heat until it renders its fat.
- Remove from skillet and drain on paper towels.
- Pour off all but 2 tablespoons of the fat from the skillet.
- Add onions and sauté stirring occasionally over medium heat about 15 minutes.
- Remove from heat and set aside.
- Grate potatoes coarsely by hand in a food processor using a coarse grating blade.
- Wash in several changes of water.
- Squeeze potatoes well in a clean linen to remove as much liquid as possible.
- Rinse and squeeze again.
- In a large bowl thoroughly combine potatoes, sautéed onions, bacon, cream, and egg yolks.
- Season generously with salt and pepper.
- Preheat oven to 375.
- Beat the egg whites until stiff then gently fold into potato mixture using a rubber spatula.
- Carefully transfer mixture to a well-buttered round baking dish or heavy oven proof skillet.
- Dot top with butter then bake 50 minutes.

269. Ultimate Baked Potato Recipe

Serving: 1 | Prep: | Cook: 75mins | Ready in:

Ingredients

- Russet or red potatoes, unpeeled.
- kosher salt.

Direction

- Move one oven rack to the lowest part of the oven and move other(s) to the top or remove.
- Place foil on bottom of oven (not on rack) to catch any dripping salt and water.
- Preheat oven to 425F.
- Thoroughly wash potatoes.
- Poke vent holes in potatoes to release steam.
- While still wet from washing coat liberally with kosher salt.
- Place salted potatoes directly on bottom rack and bake for 75 minutes.
- No peeking, keep oven door closed.
- Remove and serve piping hot with your favourite toppings.
- Toppings possibilities: butter, sour cream, chives, bacon, yogurt, finely chopped onion, feta cheese, blue cheese, goat cheese, sharp cheddar cheese, chili, olive oil, the kitchen sink.
- The most important part……ENJOY!

270. VeggieStuffed Baked Potato Recipe

Serving: 4 | Prep: | Cook: 20mins | Ready in:

Ingredients

- 1 tablespoon butter or cooking oil
- • 4 cups sliced fresh mushrooms (about 1 lb.)
- • 1 1/2 cups thinly sliced carrots
- • 1 large red pepper, cut into 1/2-inch pieces
- • 1/2 cup chopped green onions with tops
- • 1 clove garlic, minced
- • 1/4 teaspoon red pepper flakes
- • 4 eggs, beaten
- • 4 large baking potatoes, cooked

- • 1/4 cup (1 oz.) shredded reduced-fat cheddar cheese
- • Additional chopped green onion with tops, optional

Direction

- In 12-inch omelet pan over medium heat, heat butter until just hot enough to sizzle a drop of water.
- Add mushrooms, carrots, pepper, onions, garlic and pepper flakes. Cook, stirring frequently, until vegetables are crisp-tender, about 10 minutes.
- Pour in beaten eggs.
- As mixture begins to set, gently draw an inverted pancake turner completely across bottom and sides of pan, forming large soft curds.
- Continue until eggs are thickened and no visible liquid egg remains. Do not stir constantly.
- With knife, cut an "X" on top of each potato.
- Gently press lower part of potato until potato comes up through slit. Spoon 1/4 of the scrambled egg mixture into each potato.
- Sprinkle each potato with I tablespoon of the cheese and green onion, if desired.

271. Volcano Potatoe Bake Recipe

Serving: 8 | Prep: | Cook: 20mins | Ready in:

Ingredients

- 8 cps cold mashed potatoes
- 3 eggs well beaten
- 3 tbs melted butter
- 1 cp sharp cheddar cheese
- 1/4 tsp tabasco

Direction

- Make mashed potatoes ahead of time and set aside till cold (can be made the day before.
- Mound mashed potatoes on a greased baking sheet
- Form a mountain type shape and scoop a nice well in the centre
- Mix cheese, eggs and butter and tabasco
- Spoon into crater
- Bake in a 450 degree oven about 15 to 20 minutes or until potatoes have browned and filling has erupted and runs down the sides. Kids love this and so do big kids

272. Whipped Sweet Potato Bake Recipe

Serving: 10 | Prep: | Cook: 20mins | Ready in:

Ingredients

- 3 cans (15 oz. each) sweet potatoes, drained
- 1/4 cup (1/2 stick) butter, melted
- 1 tsp. ground cinnamon
- 1 tsp. ground ginger
- 1/4 tsp. ground nutmeg
- 3 cups miniature marshmallows

Direction

- HEAT oven to 350°F. Beat sweet potatoes, butter, cinnamon, ginger and nutmeg with mixer until blended.
- SPOON into lightly greased 1-1/2-qt. casserole dish; top with marshmallows.
- BAKE 15 to 20 min. or until mixture is heated through and marshmallows are lightly browned.

273. Yummy Asparagus Potato Ham Bake Recipe

Serving: 4 | Prep: | Cook: 35mins | Ready in:

Ingredients

- 1 lb. yukon gold potatoes, sliced
- 1 8-oz. tub light cream cheese spread with chive and onion
- 3/4 cup milk
- 1/4 cup finely shredded parmesan cheese
- 1 Tbsp. snipped fresh tarragon or 1/2 tsp. dried tarragon, crushed
- 8 oz. cooked boneless ham, cut in bite-sized slices
- 1 lb. fresh asparagus spears, trimmed, cut in 2 to 3-inch pieces
- tarragon sprigs (optional)

Direction

- Preheat oven to 400 degrees F. In medium saucepan cook potatoes, covered, in small amount of lightly salted boiling water 5 to 7 minutes, just until tender. Drain; transfer to bowl and set aside.
- For sauce, in same saucepan combine cream cheese, milk, 2 tablespoons Parmesan, and 1/4 teaspoon black pepper. Heat and whisk until smooth and cheese is melted. Remove from heat; stir in tarragon.
- Layer potatoes, ham, asparagus, and sauce in 1-1/2-quart baking dish. Bake, covered, 20 minutes. Uncover; sprinkle remaining Parmesan. Bake 10 to 12 minutes. Let stand 5 minutes. Top with tarragon and freshly ground black pepper. Serves 4.
- NOTE: Use small asparagus spears - big, woody ones do not work in this recipe unless you cook them a bit first.

- 1 large white onion chopped
- 6 ounces grated cheddar cheese
- 1 teaspoon chopped thyme
- 1 teaspoon chopped sage
- 1 teaspoon salt
- 1 teaspoon freshly ground black pepper
- 1/4 teaspoon nutmeg
- 2/3 cup milk

Direction

- Layer potatoes, onion, cheese, herbs and seasonings in a greased dish and pour over the milk.
- Cover and cook in a preheated 375 oven for 1 hour.
- Remove cover after 30 minutes to allow top to brown.

275. Zucchini Potato Bake Recipe

Serving: 6 | Prep: | Cook: 30mins | Ready in:

Ingredients

- 1 pound fresh zucchini, cut in chunks
- 1 small bag of Frozen, shredded, hash brown potatoes
- 1 Envelope, dry onion soup mix
- 1 can (Undiluted) mushroom or chicken SOUP
- 1 cup, shredded cheese of your choice

Direction

- DEFROST the small bag of Shredded Potatoes
- Meanwhile, Cut ZUCCHINI in Chunks
- Shred CHEESE, Save out 1/2 of the Cheese for the topping
- When POTATOES are defrosted, mix together with ALL other ingredients
- Place in a greased (or) PAM sprayed 9x9 baking dish
- Sprinkle with remaining CHEESE

274. Zooming In Potato Bake Recipe

Serving: 4 | Prep: | Cook: 60mins | Ready in:

Ingredients

- 1-1/2 pounds thinly sliced potatoes

- Bake at 350 degrees for 30 minutes, or until SQUASH is tender and it is hot and bubbly!

276. Baked Mashed Potatoes Extreme Recipe

Serving: 8 | Prep: | Cook: 45mins | Ready in:

Ingredients

- 8-10 large Idaho white potatoes
- 1 pound of sharp cheddar grated
- 4 oz of cream cheese
- 4 oz half n half
- 1 pound of smoked lean bacon
- 8 oz or frozen bell pepper mix
- 1 small red onion
- add spices to your taste

Direction

- Bake the taters it adds to the flavour,
- Cook the bacon crisp and crumble
- Sauté the peppers and onion
- Peal the taters [optional]
- gently mix in all the ingredients the cream cheese will be difficult, try not to destroy the taters to much try to leave them lumpy, use a large mixing fork mix until well blended, saving 2-3 oz. of cheddar
- Sprinkle the cheddar over the top
- Bake for 15 mins then BROIL till the top gets brown.
- This can also be used for stuffing for bell peppers,

277. Baked Potato Recipe

Serving: 1 | Prep: | Cook: 35mins | Ready in:

Ingredients

- the potatoes, can be cooked by a microwave or in the oven
- bake your clean potatoes, and slice them open
- salt them and add butter, mix it in the shell
- top with canned green chilies
- serve with chilies and butter on the table

Direction

- We will number these for you! Just hit 'enter' after every step.

278. Baked Potato Topping Recipe

Serving: 10 | Prep: | Cook: | Ready in:

Ingredients

- 1 cup sour cream
- 5 slices bacon, crispy and crumbled
- 1 tsp dried dill
- 2 tbsp fresh chives
- pinch of coarse salt
- pinch of pepper

Direction

- Mix all ingredients together
- Refrigerate for at least an hour
- Top potatoes with mixture

279. Baked Potatoe Collins Style Recipe

Serving: 2 | Prep: | Cook: 20mins | Ready in:

Ingredients

- 2 large baked potatoes.cook in micro for speed,or oven for better taste
- 4 chicken supremes ,flour egg and bread cumbed

- 12 button mushrooms fried in butter salt and black pepper
- 2oz plain flour
- 2ozbutter
- milk
- 8oz of your fav cheese grated

Direction

- Butter in pan add the flour make a roux, add the milk. Get a nice creamy coating texture, add the cheese
- Cook the chicken and mushrooms
- Split the cooked hot potatoes
- Put the chicken and mushrooms in the centre
- Cover with the sauce grill for a few mins and serve. I could eat it now
- Regards

280. Baked Whipped Cheezy Potatoes Recipe

Serving: 68 | Prep: | Cook: 120mins |Ready in:

Ingredients

- 1-head garlic- oven roasted, O.K. cook up 2-3, cause you know you wanna
- 4- green onions diced/chopped
- 6-8 fist sized potatoes
- 1/4 C. butter
- 1/2 C. sour cream
- 3/4C. milk
- 3/4 C. old / sharp cheddar cheese

Direction

- cut the tips off of the garlic heads, place in baking dish ,drizzle olive oil about a tbsp. over each head, cover dish with lid , bake in a 350 degree oven for about 1 hr. or until cloves are soft when poked with a fork. Remove from oven & let cool
- Wash, peel, & cut up potatoes, place into pot boil till ready to be mashed
- I mash potatoes with a hand masher first, then add butter, milk, sour cream & 1/2C, of the cheese,
- I then use an electric hand mixer to whip the potatoes & above ingredients together.
- Fold in the green onions
- Put whipped potatoes into a greased Pyrex baking dish
- Sprinkle remaining cheddar over potatoes, cover & bake for 1/2 hr. @ 350
- Remove lid put oven on broil till cheese bubbles 2-3 min.
- Serve immediately
- Any leftovers, make a great start to my killer - cream of leek soup

281. Caramalised Onion And Cheese Potato Bake Recipe

Serving: 4 | Prep: | Cook: 45mins |Ready in:

Ingredients

- 2 onions
- butter
- sugar
- 4 potatoes
- cream/milk
- chedder cheese
- salt and pepper

Direction

- Peel potatoes and boil till tender enough to mash.
- Whilst potatoes are boiling, slice onions and fry them in butter for about 10 mins until soft and slightly coloured.
- Add as much sugar as you want to the onions and cook for about 5 mins until onions coated and caramalised.
- Spoon 3/4 of the onions into the bottom of ovenproof dish.

- Once potatoes are cooked, drain and mash with some more butter if you wish and either cream or milk till desired consistency.
- Season potatoes to preferred taste and spoon in remaining onions. Add cheese to potatoes and stir well.
- Spoon potato mix over the onions in ovenproof dish and top with more cheese. Put in oven until cheese melted.
- Also great with crispy bacon added to the potato and garlic.

282. Cheesy Potato And Ham Bake Recipe

Serving: 6 | Prep: | Cook: 20mins | Ready in:

Ingredients

- 1/2 bag of frozen hashbrowns (total of 16 oz.)
- 1 cup sour cream
- 1 cup milk
- 2 tbsp. flour
- 6 ounces cheddar cheese, sliced
- 2 tsp. garlic powder
- 4 ounces ham
- 1/4 yellow onion, diced
- 1 cup broccoli florettes

Direction

- Preheat oven to 425
- Pour hash browns in the bottom of a casserole dish
- Mix together milk, sour cream, flour, onions, and garlic powder
- Chop up the ham into bite size pieces and sprinkle over the potatoes, along with broccoli
- Top with slices of cheese.
- Pour sour cream mixture over the entire dish
- Bake for 20 minutes

283. Cheesy Potato Bake Recipe

Serving: 4 | Prep: | Cook: 45mins | Ready in:

Ingredients

- 2 can cream of broccoli
- 2 can cream of cheddar cheese
- 6 potatoes
- 1 package cheddarworsts (or sausage of choice)
- 1 casserole dish, with top

Direction

- Preheat oven to 375
- Cut potatoes into 2in squares and triangles
- Cut sausage into 2 in pieces
- Mix potatoes, sausage, and cans evenly into casserole dish and cover
- Bake until potatoes are tender
- Let cool for 5 minutes to thicken
- Serve and enjoyed

284. Garlic Lovers Baked Potato Recipe

Serving: 1 | Prep: | Cook: 1mins | Ready in:

Ingredients

- baking potato
- lawry's garlic salt

Direction

- Rinse/clean potato of any debris. Pierce potato to prevent explosion. While potato is damp, sprinkle Lawry's garlic salt (best garlic salt on market, only garlic salt I do not have allergic reactions from) on entire potato. Bake at 400 degrees, for 1 hour, turning at 20 minute intervals. Slice potato lengthwise and also down side of potato at 1/2 inch intervals (about 1/2 - 1 inch down side of potato). Top w/ favourite toppings and mix into potato. Peel off potato leaves, dip into potato, or eat plain and enjoy.

285. Ham And Cheese Potato Bake Recipe

Serving: 4 | Prep: | Cook: 1mins | Ready in:

Ingredients

- 1 package frozen O'Brien hash brown potatoes
- 2 cups cubed ham
- 1 bag shredded cheddar cheese
- 1 small onion, chopped
- 1 can sour cream
- 1 can condensed cheddar cheese soup, undiluted
- 1 can condensed cream of potato soup, undiluted
- 1/4 teaspoon pepper

Direction

- Combine potatoes, ham, 1/2 cheese and onion.
- In another bowl, combine sour cream, soups and pepper; add to potato mixture and mix well.
- Transfer to a greased 3-qt. baking dish.
- Sprinkle with remaining cheese.
- Bake at 350° for 60-65 minutes or until bubbly and potatoes are tender.
- Let stand for 10 minutes before serving.

Index

A
Anchovies 4,50
Apple 3,4,5,6,34,38,59,63,64,113
Asparagus 7,119

B
Bacon 3,4,5,18,37,38,48,50,57,62,76
Baking 8,13
Beef 3,4,13,61
Beer 36
Berry 6,114
Bread 4,5,48,85,86
Brie 124
Broccoli 3,5,23,62
Butter 3,4,5,6,8,21,29,34,39,55,59,64,87,106,110,122

C
Cake 3,6,32,111,112
Caramel 5,64
Carrot 4,5,38,39,78
Cashew 5,79
Cheddar 3,5,15,18,21,25,26,27,53,57,65,85,89,91,95,108
Cheese 3,4,5,6,7,21,23,35,37,48,53,57,60,62,65,66,69,74,76,79,80,85,94,96,110,112,117,120,122,124
Cherry 64
Chicken 3,4,5,6,27,39,66,67,75,78,81,87,88,99
Chilli 5,68
Chips 4,54
Chives 4,8,28,48
Chorizo 5,69

Cinnamon 4,55
Crab 3,4,10,51
Cream 4,5,6,27,60,65,71,72,74,85,95,102,103,105,110,115
Crumble 22,74

D
Date 6,7,107,117
Dijon mustard 35,42,76,97
Dill 4,6,40,95

E
Egg 3,4,5,6,11,40,41,44,75,102

F
Fat 5,77,85
Feta 4,5,51,80
Fish 4,5,6,58,80,110
Fontina cheese 72,76,117
French bread 69

G
Garlic 4,5,6,7,28,60,68,83,105,106,107,123
Gin 4,57
Gouda 26,27,33,72,89
Gratin 5,6,71,89
Gravy 6,94

H
Ham 4,5,6,7,53,85,101,102,119,123,124
Herbs 6,97,108
Honey 4,5,57,87
Horseradish 8

J
Jus 26,46,103,121

K
Kale 19

L

Lemon 6,90

Lime 6,90

Lobster 3,15

M

Macaroni 5,79

Margarine 59

Milk 19,85

Mince 28,81

Mint 6,96

Mozzarella 93

Mushroom 3,4,6,10,50,65,97

Mustard 4,6,42,59,97

N

Nut 4,39,70,86

O

Oil 82,110

Olive 4,51,73,82,110

Onion 3,5,7,9,32,43,59,64,65,77,81,84,86,94,122

Oregano 28

P

Pancakes 5,70

Parmesan 4,9,29,50,52,68,73,75,85,89,93,94,95,102,107,108,112,117,120

Parsley 5,28,62,76

Peanuts 4,42

Peel 24,39,46,49,56,59,67,70,72,80,81,87,90,117,122,124

Pepper 3,5,28,75,82,105

Pie 3,12,13,15,16,23,27,30,37,51,64,77,83,84,91,123

Pineapple 6,114

Pizza 4,6,44,91

Pork 64

Potato 1,3,4,5,6,7,8,9,10,11,12,13,14,15,16,17,18,19,20,21,22,23,24,25,26,27,28,29,30,31,32,33,34,35,37,38,39,40,41,42,43,44,45,46,47,48,49,50,51,52,53,54,55,56,57,58,59,60,61,62,63,64,65,66,67,68,69,70,71,72,73,74,75,76,77,78,79,80,81,82,83,84,85,86,87,88,89,90,91,92,93,94,95,96,97,98,99,100,101,102,103,104,105,106,107,108,109,110,111,112,113,114,115,116,117,118,119,120,121,122,123,124

R

Ricotta 91

Rosemary 3,6,20,105

S

Sage 3,4,25,50,59

Salad 4,6,41,42,45,49,59,91,95

Salmon 6,105

Salt 6,8,9,16,40,45,50,59,63,106,110

Sardine 5,77

Sausage 5,6,67,106

Savory 6,107

Scallop 6,89

Seasoning 43,64,89,108

Smoked cheese 110

Smoked fish 110

Soup 4,21,27,47,65

Spices 16

Spinach 3,4,6,15,29,50,111,112

Stuffing 4,38

Sumac 6,50,96

T

Tabasco 46

Taco 4,6,47,115

Tea 59

Tomato 4,58

Turkey 5,6,64,86,116

V

Vegetable oil 43,70

W
Walnut 5,74
Y
Yam 3,26,31

Conclusion

Thank you again for downloading this book!

I hope you enjoyed reading about my book!

If you enjoyed this book, please take the time to share your thoughts and post a review on Amazon. It'd be greatly appreciated!

Write me an honest review about the book – I truly value your opinion and thoughts and I will incorporate them into my next book, which is already underway.

Thank you!

If you have any questions, **feel free to contact at:** *author@fetarecipes.com*

Penny Patton

fetarecipes.com